Wounded Warriors

SURVIVING SEASONS OF STRESS

R. Loren Sandford

VICTORY HOUSE PUBLISHERS
Tulsa, Oklahoma

Unless otherwise identified, all Scripture quotations are taken from the *King James Version* of the Bible.

WOUNDED WARRIORS
ISBN 0–932081–17–7
Copyright © 1987 by R. Loren Sandford

Published by Victory House, Inc.
P.O. Box 700238
Tulsa, Oklahoma 74170

Printed in the United States of America

Contents

Prologue

Shortly after I completed this manuscript, I taught one half-hour of a three-hour seminar entitled "Different Approaches to Healing," at the North American Leaders' Congress on the Holy Spirit and World Evangelization in New Orleans. My subject was "Wounded Warriors" and, as usual, I focused my talk on leaders.

Afterwards, I was overwhelmed by people who wanted to speak to me, not by pastors and leaders, but by housewives who had suffered through divorces, by businessmen who had struggled to survive, by laypeople who had been driven from their churches because of differences of opinion with leadership and by others who had suffered stress from any number of other sources. They thanked me for speaking to their experience in a way no one had shared before.

Originally, I wrote the manuscript for this book with leaders in mind, but, until New Orleans, I didn't fully realize that neither the symptoms of, nor the solutions for, stress exhaustion are unique to those in leadership positions. As a result, what I have to say concerning wounded leaders ministers to almost everyone since most people have at some time experienced different kinds of stress overloads.

I, therefore, considered revising the manuscript to speak more directly to the wider Body of Christ but decided not to. To do so would make what I intended to be refreshingly brief and simple into an intolerably long document from the point of view of one who is wounded. This work ministers to leaders and lay-people alike without any alterations.

One brief illustration completes my point. A brilliant graduate student in a field not directly related to Christian leadership stumbled into my office. She'd left school in a state of collapse, unable to work. Her self-image and self-respect were a complete shambles. I gave her the unpublished manuscript of this book to read because I perceived that her physical and emotional problems were symptoms of stress exhaustion.

At her next appointment I asked her how she liked it. She responded, "It was like sitting down and talking to a friend who understood exactly everything I was feeling."

It is my prayer that you will experience the same feeling of empathy from these pages, and that, as a result, God will bring healing to you and to those who are under your care.

R. Loren Sandford
Post Falls, Idaho

Song for a Wounded Warrior

When I draw upon my inner well and find
no water there,
And reach into the pantry where the cupboards
all are bare,
My feet are torn and bleeding from the glass
strewn in my way,
Then I pray the long night changes
To the brightness of your day, Lord!

When I flee before my enemies, turn and find
no one was there,
Nursing secret terrors no other man can share,
I'd come into your throne room, but I cannot
find the door,
Then I pray you, Lord, to find me,
For your heart bleeds for the poor, Lord!

Jesus! Jesus! You are my only hope!

I've heard the desperate murmur of a thousand
wandering souls,
But I've learned you're where my home is,
And that keeps me from the cold.
And you've reserved a place for me,
And you've given me your name,
And I know the long night changes to the
brightness of your day, Lord!

Jesus! Jesus! You are my only hope!

Introduction

A middle-aged pastor of a dynamic and growing, multi-staff congregation sat before me in my office. His face was ashen-gray and his eyes were vaguely unfocused. I noted a subtle shaking of his hands. As I pointed this out to him, he related, "I can work only two hours a day before the shaking becomes unbearable." I later learned that counseling situations with parishioners caused a swelling of his sinuses and overwhelming drowsiness. The ringing of the telephone would strike fear into him like a knife slicing through his heart. Sundays were an exercise in survival and God only knows how he found the strength to prepare and deliver a message each week. He had made it to that point only with the help of the pills the doctor prescribed.

The prayer closet became a place of fear for him rather than a sanctuary of peace. To enter into the quiet place with God was synonymous with facing an almost unbearable mountain of despair and a hopeless sense of abandonment and alienation. In the congregation, word of his weakness began to spread. As a result, the "sharks" began to circle, wagging their tongues of criticism as the blood from their wounded leader excited their instinct to attack. Every mistake he made was magnified by the weak and unbalanced members of the flock. The pastor's paranoia ran rampant as he sensed the stirring of the troublemakers. His ability to maintain his tenuous grip on reality wore thinner by the day. How can I possibly help him? I wondered.

This small book had its beginning at a seminar in Spokane, Washington, entitled, "Healing the Wounded Warrior." My wife, Beth, and I led the discussion along with other members of the Elijah House team. This book is not the product of extensive psychological or statistical research, but is, rather, the fruit of my own experiences. When I examine my own experiences in the light of God's Word, I am often able to see patterns common to others and then apply them in ministry.

I'm not a psychologist. I'm just a pastor who counsels. My qualification for writing this book is that I, myself, was a Wounded Warrior who went all the way to the bottom, emotionally and physically, and experienced a substantial healing. I've counseled a number of others like me and I've found considerable commonality in the suffering, causes and recovery we've shared.

The subject touches me deeply, not only because of my personal experience, but because I suspect that the great majority of pastors, and even of high-profile lay leaders in our local churches, have at some time experienced a depth of wounding or burn-out that has threatened not only their capacity to minister, but even their ability to deal with daily life.

Surviving such seasons of stress can be very difficult indeed. Very little real help is available. Few counselors truly understand the problem. The sufferer has often been to his family doctor for any number of associated physical symptoms and has been given a clean bill of health. This has left him confused and discouraged because the aches, pains and ills he is experiencing are very real and truly do hinder his ability to function adequately.

The "faith" and "success in life" teachings currently in vogue are cruel medicine to such wounded ones who already feel as if they're failing, and many have reached such a point of emotional and physical weakness that they are unable to accomplish what these teachings call them to perform, no matter how hard they try. They simply can't "believe" any longer or "confess" positively as they ought.

Such teachings only make them feel accused. They're filled with fear that their fatigue, anxiety and pain will be exposed and condemned, and these teachings often have a way of visiting condemnation on those who suffer from fear, fatigue and anxiety. Their faith has been shaken and shattered and it's no help to have that shakiness accentuated. They have sunk to a depth from which they can no longer lift themselves by any corrective effort of right thinking or acting. Some of them have been beaten to the point that they can't even believe emotionally that God personally loves them any more.

From time to time the inner pressure of despair combines with the outer pressure of the ministry to produce a devastating breakdown. The shockwaves then reverberate through the Body of Christ—which usually reacts, not with Christian compassion, but with back-stabbing and comments like, "I told you there was something wrong in that ministry!" All too often it seems that when our leaders stumble, we bite and devour, rather than pray for and heal them.

It is my sincere hope to play a part in awakening the Body of Christ to a crisis in the Church that is already epidemic. Please, God, let us develop compassionate understanding for those in leadership positions in the Body of Christ. I desperately want us to know how to minister—and how *not* to minister—to Wounded Warriors.

But most of all, I want to speak to those who are themselves wounded, fearful and teetering on the brink of collapse, both clergy and lay leaders. I want to say that you are not alone, that you are not hopeless and that neither your sins nor your inadequacies are necessarily the cause of what is happening to you. *You have not lost your anoint-*

ing.

Having shared the manuscript with a number of people, both Wounded Warriors and those stressed out due to other causes, I have found this small book to be helpful for more folks than the title suggests. Anyone who has suffered long-term stress from any cause can find something useful here.

I've tried to write simply and briefly because I know that those in deep wounding can no longer tolerate complexities and lengthy periods of study. Even small tasks often appear to be insurmountable obstacles. I speak from my heart because I know that the wounded among us can hear that sort of word and be lifted by it. I speak from my heart because the deeply wounded can no longer find their answers in theology or in method, no matter how eternally true or logically practical these may be. Such are food for healthy people, but I am speaking for the sake of those who have sacrificed their emotional and physical well-being in the service of their Lord. Those who have hit the bottom can no longer think or do as others can, and no amount of new learning or self-help will fix them. A special kind of mercy and grace is called for. They must be lifted and carried in a tender way that gives much and asks little.

I've couched everything in masculine terms, as if all Wounded Warriors are males. This is only for the sake of convenience and because that is the nature of my own experience. I was wounded, and

I am male. I realize it is possible to be female and wounded in the same ways and I trust the reader to be able to apply the principles wherever they are appropriate.

I would like to express my gratitude to the elders of Cornerstone (our church) and their wives: Mike and Karen Gerken, Jim and Marcia Tiffany, Cliff and Audrey Wagner, Jeff and Sue Guyett and Larry and Nancy Cron (who have since moved away). These people supported me in my weakness and carried more than their share of the load while I walked the path of the wounded. Having fought the same battles I did, some of them are now in the process of recovering from the casualty list.

Most of all, I thank the angel whom God sent to be my life's partner. Beth's gentle nature and stubborn joy are a major reason I came through it all intact.

Chapter 1

Three Kinds of Damage

1

Three Kinds of Damage

Burn-out has become a common term in the last decade or so. Its use is reflective of a heightened awarenesss of a widespread problem common among those who expend themselves in the service of others. In my view, this condition actually involves three kinds of damage, of which burn-out is only one. Depression and wounding are the other two.

For the present purpose I'll differentiate burn-out from depression and wounding by saying that burn-out happens only to givers. Its nature is the depletion of the physical and emotional resources that enable the giver to keep giving. The loss of these resources leads to despair, depression, irrational anger and a host of physical problems. Burn-outs are those who have too little consciousness of—or care for—their personal needs to do what is necessary to replenish themselves from the intensity of their giving. Frequently a period of rest will cure burn-out; the same is often not true of depression and wounding.

Depression is an emotional manifestation of the depletion of one's physical and emotional resources for dealing with stress and can happen to anyone, giver or not, who faces and inadequately deals with stress over a period of time. In its most extreme form, depression may be so debilitating that the victim almost completely loses the ability to function and cannot in any way summon up enough initiative to get moving with life again. For such people, hopelessness becomes their total environment.

Depression is often the result of one's performance orientation. Performance-oriented people have not learned that they are acceptable apart from what they can achieve. For the performance-oriented person, the hope of love and the ability to accept oneself always center about meeting the expectations of self or others for behavior or productivity. Unfortunately, this fear motivation for living and achieving exacts a terrible physical and emotional toll. The result can be deep depression until the victim learns that self-acceptance, the love of God and the love of others come by grace, and are totally unearned.

Wounding is an emotional condition caused by the hurtful acts of others. I've discovered that just as the body has finite and exhaustible physical resources through which it copes with life, so our emotions draw upon limited resources in human strength in order to meet and deal with the lumps life serves up for the heart. When those resources are spent, the result is devastation and desperation. Anyone can suffer emotional wounding, but the wounding is especially severe for those who are givers by nature or by profession.

It simply won't do to talk about professional detachment at this point. In order for people to be healed, there must be a meeting of persons, and in any meeting of persons, there is a risking of oneself, a necessary level of vulnerability. Therefore, when one for whom you have poured forth your life turns on you with fangs bared, the pain can be excruciating and the expenditure of emotional and physical energy required to deal with it can be enormous.

Normally, life serves up its hurts, betrayals and abandonments by loved ones at a pace that leaves time for recovery and replenishment, but occasionally they come either too quickly or hurt too deeply for the individual to recover from them effectively. The result is wreckage in the form of physical illness, depression, withdrawal, paranoia and fear of emotional risk.

Obviously, there are significant areas of overlapping and interrelationships between burn-out, depression and wounding, both in causes and effects. I have differentiated between burn-out, wounding and depression in this chapter only to emphasize that the condition I'm ultimately addressing is more serious and more complex than the kind of thing many of us have become accustomed to reading about in professional journals.

The pain suffered by so many is clearly deeper than can be accounted for by the mere depletion of energies. Likewise, the remedies involve much more than just rearranging schedules and re-prioritizing activities. Having made this point, I will henceforth use the terms "burn-out," "wounding" and their derivatives interchangeably.

For the sake of discussion, I have divided the process of degeneration into three stages. Each of these stages, in turn, is examined in three sections: the first describing the physical symptoms evident at that stage, the second addressing the emotional condition of the sufferer and the third suggesting what sort of ministry can be appropriately offered by those who wish to help.

Chapter 2

Stage 1 Wounding: Onset

2

Stage 1 Wounding: Onset

Physical Symptoms

In the early stages of wounding or burn-out, the sufferer may feel chronic fatigue and noticeably increased recovery times following severe exertions of time and energy. Crises such as funerals or commitments (such as leading a youth camp for a week) begin to take discouragingly long periods of time to recover from. Whereas the individual may have recovered quickly, in the past, from extra energy expenditures by "sleeping-in" for a day or two, he now needs a week or more to feel really right again.

Tired people make more mistakes than healthy ones. As one in the early stages of burn-out grows more fatigued, he will find himself committing more errors, especially in relationships with others. This will take place most especially in sensitive relationships that are important to maintain for the health of the ministry. Because he sometimes doesn't hear all that is said to him, through the veil of his fatigue, he may occasionally respond in inappropriate ways to those who come to him with questions and needs. He may mean to tease a friend in a loving way, but have it come out sounding like a hurtful insult. He may forget to include important people in the plans he makes for the ministry and then suffer their hurt and/or wrath for his error.

All of this feeds the poisonous tongues that are always ready to wag in the church and adds to the burden of stress that has begun to drag him down. Some may begin to assign evil motives to his actions and to accuse him of not loving them or of being insensitive to the needs of others. Such talk creates a spiritual pressure on his ministry that tends to lock up the anointing and hinder his effectiveness. Even Jesus couldn't do many miracles in His hometown because of the unbelief of the people living there. The Wounded Warrior knows more deeply than anyone else the meaning of what Jesus faced.

More and more frequently he doesn't feel good about getting up in the morning. Refreshment eludes him and there are whole days when he feels unexplainably and uncharacteristically sleepy and he must push himself to keep moving.

Falling asleep is increasingly difficult, and rarely is the night restful when he finally does nod off. His mind won't let go of things and races on uncontrolled. At first he may pass it off by saying, "I do my most creative thinking in bed before I go to sleep." It's probably true, but in later stages, the creativity will die out, while the wake-fulness continues tearing at him night after night. Dreams are increasingly troubled in their content and occur more frequently, leaving him exhausted in the morning as if he'd been working all night.

He begins to notice physical-tension reac-tions. My personal "favorite" is what I call "lock-jaw." It's a wonder my teeth survive the pressure. Others may notice increasing and chronic muscle tension in the shoulders or other areas. Nervous tappings of the hands and feet may appear. Twitching of muscles in the face or elsewhere may become habitual. Headaches may increase in fre-quency and intensity.

For many of us, tension tends to express itself through the digestive system. The beginnings of colitis may appear as chronic pain in the lower ab-domen, or as recurring bouts with irregularities in bowel movements—or both.

Emotional Condition

More than anything else, there may be an in-creasing consciousness of fear or anxiety—not at-tributable to any known cause except when it can be attached to a coming situation in which perfor-mance is called for. At this stage, such anxiety is still just background noise that can be eclipsed by the intensity of ministry or other activities. For many of us such fear may even be an effective tool for enhanced performance because of the slight adrenalin edge it gives, but this benefit will pass. I promise. This anxiety may be identified as fear of failure, fear of the unknown, fear of attack or any other sort of fear, but my point is that the ability to deal with it, and to subdue it, has begun to erode.

In the early stages of wounding, more and more nagging questions arise concerning one's faith and his personal relationship with God. These questions don't seem to have answers. The wounded one asks, "Is the counseling I'm doing really effective? Will I really receive or achieve the things God has promised me? Will the problems ever be solvable? Is God really here for me?" Yet, in spite of the fear and the questioning, he still hopes deeply and is able to encourage others with that hope. The disturbing thing is that his ability to live creatively with the questions is beginning to weaken.

His prayer life remains intact. Daily devotions remain a place of refreshment and of conversation with God, but he begins to wonder at the frequency of dry spots. Perhaps more significantly, fatigue, the pressure of daily life and the demands of people for his personal ministry begin to cut into his prayer time and he feels helpless to stop it.

At this stage he still has confidence in his ability, anointing and strength, if confidence and strength were what he began his ministry with. I can remember that my wife warned me repeatedly about the quantity of energy I was expending. I would answer, "I have a course to run,

Beth, and I don't have God's permission to stop yet. The job isn't done." We were involved in starting a new church, laying foundations, building people and all that comes with the task of carving a body of Christ out of the spiritual wilderness. Today, on the recovery side of wounding, I know I was right and that I would say the same thing again. But I also know that the *spirit* of my reply would be different. You who've been there know what I mean.

In this period of time the anointing of the Lord does sustain you in spite of fatigue, but more and more often you run on adrenalin strength, sometimes not knowing the difference between adrenalin rush and the anointing of God. Understanding the difference is a function of wisdom, and wisdom is won only through suffering.

In stage one, the individual entering upon burn-out begins to shave such activities as recreation and exercise from his schedule. He may even feel a bit noble about it, glorying in the sense that he is wearing himself out in the service of the Lord. And it's true; he really does love the Lord, but work and its related stresses leave little energy for fun and personal replenishment. The care of his physical "temple" suffers.

Time away from the work still recharges his batteries and reenergizes his creativity, but he is ever more disturbed at how quickly his emotional reserves dissipate after he returns. He begins to wonder how long he would have to be away in order to come back fully recovered.

Ministry to Stage One

At this point, normal ministry is still possible. A stage-one wounded warrior can still engage in the kind of interaction with others that is so necessary to most healing. You can talk with him concerning root causes of his condition and he can respond, recognize his sin and pray wonderfully well in relation to it. You can pray for his deliverance and he'll shed tears and thank you for it. But don't expect much fruit. Most likely he already knows what must be done to turn his condition around and either can't or won't do it.

As I was, by this time he's probably locked into a set of self-destructive patterns that are too strong to be easily or quickly broken. He will likely have to ride them to the bottom before their power is defeated in his life. He'll have to burn out on being burned out.

I myself knew I had a task to perform from which I couldn't turn aside and in which I felt I had too little real help. The pressure of that task prevented me from slowing down long enough to deal with the issue of my own needs in a life-changing way. Real healing was impossible until the course had been run and the task was finished. The finishing nearly finished me.

It seems to me that conventional wisdom focuses on preventing burn-out from occurring. I'm not certain this is always the wisest approach. I'm not all that interested in preventing burn-out because I'm convinced that the condition is a tool of the Lord for crucifying His servants unto new life.

In burn-out old patterns are burned away, along with old attitudes and fleshly ways of approaching life and its inhabitants. Even had I known how to stop my downward slide in its early stages, I probably wouldn't have done it, because all along I had the sense that it was the hand of God leading me down this path and that if I simply embraced the pain I would learn wisdom. I was right. Jesus is Lord.

I was about to enter upon what is often known as "the long, dark night of the soul." Especially if you are a dynamic personality, you enter upon your ministry filled with talents and abilities and endowed with boundless energy to make those talents and abilities effective in ministry. In the beginning you aren't wise or experienced enough to know the difference between anointing and natural strength, but it isn't yet important for you to know this because the name of the game at this point is growth and knowledge.

Then, when it seems you have it all together and that everything you touch turns to gold because of the anointing of God and the wisdom He's taught you, God takes it all away. Nothing works any more. God seems far away and you begin to question everything you thought you knew. God has taken you to the cross and there is no escape until you know you have nothing and He has all, until the flesh is burned away and the Spirit makes you alive. Until that point, all you can do is hold your heart open to the searingly bright light of His presence and endure the pain His purity creates in your flesh and brokenness.

Finally, when you can endure no more, when the cross has done its work, our Lord restores all that you lost, but now it's no longer yours but His. And you know it more deeply than you ever thought possible.

Therefore, I'm not interested in prevention because I'm not interested in preserving the flesh. This is a suffering to be embraced, accepted and seen through to its end. Though he may not know it, the stage-one Wounded Warrior is still running hard in his natural strength, and God is about to bring it to an end.

Chapter 3

Stage 2 Wounding:
Breakdown Begins

3

Stage 2 Wounding: Breakdown Begins

Physical Symptoms

Adrenal burn-out begins. I'm not a physician. I know only what those who care professionally for my body tell me. Adrenal burn-out occurs when the adrenal gland has overproduced for such a long time that it can no longer function as it was designed to function. Whereas stress once created an adrenalin "rush" that could be used to enhance performance, it now often produces a sensation of sickness, like trying to start a car in cold weather on a dead battery.

In fact, the sufferer has become stress-addicted. He actually subconsciously needs and creates stressful work situations so that the fear, the pressure and the resulting adrenalin production overcome his fatigue. But adrenalin no longer gets him moving like it once did. The "rush" is gone. Sometimes it makes him sick and angry.

For example, from time to time I used to find

myself in unexpected possession of a free day for sermon preparation early in the week, and then almost subconsciously find some way of filling up that free time so that I would be "under the gun" on Saturday. Given a light load, I produced mediocre work, but given an overload, I worked like a madman at the peak of my form and excellence. I *needed* stress in order to function, and without it, I went to sleep from fatigue. One of the recovering alcoholics in our congregation asked me once if I was addicted to adrenalin flow. I had to answer yes.

At stage two in the process of degeneration, stress addiction begins to fail as a motivator and fatigue is taken for granted as an unpleasant fact of life. Burn-out victims then find it difficult to remember or even to imagine life without exhaustion.

Digestive disturbances are common, attacking whatever is the weakest link in the system. The wounded one may develop ulcers. Colitis may flair up and cause extreme pain. Food allergies may appear. Diarrhea is common. This is because the digestive system reacts to stress by producting more acid and other chemicals than the system was designed for with the result that it becomes overly sensitive to minor irritants.

Not only is sleep occasionally difficult, it becomes a labor. I remember dreaming night after night that I was in a battle in which I had no power over my enemy. Every movement was like swimming through molasses, my every stroke deprived of power. Or I might find myself in combat without my sword and swinging frantically at my enemy with an imaginary one. After a night of fruitless warfare I would awaken, drained and sick. Sleeping became so difficult that I would stay up late partly in order to reach such a point of fatigue that I knew I would sleep quickly and soundly.

In general, physical illness becomes more common. Colds come more frequently and stay longer. Aches and pains proliferate. Sore throats develop several times each year and take ages to recover from. Headaches increase in frequency and intensity.

The sufferer may notice that his physical-tension reactions to ministry situations have intensified. My sinuses would swell shut and my eyes would feel as if they wanted to cross whenever I faced an afternoon of counseling appointments. They'd become so heavy with sleep that I would catch myself nodding off in the midst of someone's tear-filled account of terrible woe and I would cry out desperately to God to please make it end. I finally discovered that if I loaded up on caffeine from the coffee pot before I began my counseling day, I could make it through. But that caused bad side effects, too, as well as diminishing returns.

Emotional Condition

Fear becomes nearly constant and is harder to ignore. At this stage, the sufferer may be plagued with thoughts that the ministry will fail and that things are going wrong in ways he is powerless to correct. From where will the next blow fall? Betrayals and fears appear larger than life and his perspective is restored only by a major exercise of mental discipline.

For example, I have a burden-bearer's nature. That means I can sense in my spirit how our church is doing at any given time, instinctively knowing when there is discord or trouble, even when I'm two thousand miles away on a speaking trip. During this period in my wounding, I could sense when poisonous tongues began to wag and I would be afraid in a way that I no longer had the capacity to control. I still had the strength to govern how I responded to it, but I couldn't control its intensity.

I sensed when personal attacks were developing and was doubly wounded by reason of fear when they actually materialized. I even began to be afraid that my anointing would expire, although it never did and God never let me down. Road trips for speaking engagements around the country became welcome respites from pressure in the home ministry. At home I felt powerless, but in foreign places overwhelmingly positive responses from people restored my flagging sense of anointing.

At last the wounded one's confidence is threatened. He begins to feel as if he is ministering from an empty bucket that isn't being refilled. Desperation takes root as again and again he goes to the well for strength and wisdom to meet the needs of others and finds nothing to draw upon.

As he loses perspective on the significance of failures and setbacks, he finds himself unable to take encouragement from successes as he once did. In fact, he may become functionally blind to the goodness in his ministry.

Ministry becomes pure pain, interspersed with brief episodes of joy and sanity. He finds himself growing more and more angry with those who ask for his time and energy, most especially with the ubiquitous church "leeches" who consume vast amounts of time and energy for little apparent return or purpose.

Episodes of withdrawal come more and more frequently, with heightened intensity and extended duration. He withdraws even from family and friends, since he has no energy left with which to deal with demands of any kind. In this condition, even offers of love may come to him as demands that he must respond to in some way so that, instead of feeling refreshed by the love of those close to him, he may feel drained by it.

People around him in the ministry may add to his wounding by complaining that he doesn't seem as warm as he once did. For example, circumstances may prevent him from being present for a crisis or two, and that becomes a reason for the victims of the crisis to attack him in private conversation.

He begins to wonder angrily if his people would be satisfied if he gashed himself and gave them his very blood. If his normal nature is to be physically affectionate, people may begin to feel that his hugs aren't as real as they once were. It may be apparent that he doesn't listen as well as he used to. All this may provoke talk in the fellowship that will add to his stress.

He may begin to stay up late in order to find time alone. In my own case, having both an acute spiritual awareness and a burden-bearing nature, I can feel the people to whom I minister drawing on me spiritually until about 10:00 PM, when they begin to go to bed. At that hour I can actually sense them letting go of me and by 11:00 PM I'm blissfully alone in every way.

When I'm in my withdrawal mode, those late night hours become *my* time. But it's a self-defeating pattern because morning doesn't come any later, and my sleep hours are accordingly abbreviated. Others in this condition perhaps go to bed early and get up early for the same reason. The wounded one feels driven to find that time in solitude.

Episodes of rage at God become common. The second stage burn-out feels abandoned and betrayed by Him. In his eyes God hasn't been a protector. God hasn't kept His promises to him and never will. He feels as though God is there for others through him, but seldom for him personally. God has let him down.

Our church is five years old. In the beginning, God gave us a number of promises concerning growth and ministry, but rather than fulfill them immediately, He gave us a double dose of troublemakers who went right to work attacking me and distorting my words and actions. When they couldn't find something to distort, they'd make things up, and along the way they'd convince themselves that what they made up was true. So, until they left, we got nowhere as a congregation in terms of realizing the promises of God for our church.

Later, I understood what a time of laying foundations that was and how precious all the wisdom I learned was, but while it was happening it didn't seem that way. It seemed then that if the Lord said to make room for all the growth He would give us, the next Sunday would see a record low attendance for the year!

Because of the betrayals by people and God's delay in fulfilling promises, I experienced episodes of such deep wounding that I began to call God a liar, betrayer and promise-breaker. I told Him not to promise me anything any more because I couldn't stand the pain of being let down again.

Needless to say, prayer life suffers at this stage and becomes a roller-coaster of ups and downs. Sometimes God comes through in prayer with such blessing that you feel like a fool for all the anger you felt. But more and more the prayer closet becomes a place of pain and alienation, a place to remember God hasn't kept His promises and that He has not protected you from the strife of tongues. As a result, you pray less.

The wounded one in stage two can still hope—and does so in blessed episodes of light and freedom—but the ability to do so is fading fast. Periods of despair are common and almost paralyzing. He finds himself subject to sudden impulses to weep over silly things.

One of the jokes in my family is how I hate children's features like "Winnie the Pooh" and "101 Dalmatians." We have a friendly family teasing session every time such a movie comes on the television and I am forced to watch it with my kids.

At this point in my downward slide, however, I could be found in the late-night hours secretly tuning in to the Disney Channel and sniffling over the sorrows of some ridiculous cartoon character, wondering what on earth was the matter with me. Actually, I had begun to store up unresolved hurts and tensions that could be tapped into and made to overflow by unlikely stimuli.

Creativity in ministry is affected because there just isn't enough energy, enthusiasm or faith left to think up new things. That builds fear for the future of the work, and the fear only adds to the problem. Creative, artistic temperaments need "down" time in which to recharge, times when the mind is allowed to work at its own pace, unbullied, until it naturally generates something new and fresh. When it does, there is a sense of relief, release and lifting that beats dozens of hours of counseling for the refreshment it brings. Stage-two Wounded Warriors find their "down" time invaded and stolen and they feel powerless to stop it. The result is a build-up of tension with no avenue of release.

One's sex life may begin to suffer because emotionally he can no longer function in the give and take of relationships, and because, physically, he's too weak to generate much libido. That can lead to stress in a marriage, which, in turn, adds to the problem.

Beth and I never stumbled in our marriage, but it was evident that in my withdrawal I wasn't giving my wife as much affection, either in public or in private, as I once did. Beth and I had had a happy marriage, and she fully understood where I was, giving me the room to withdraw as I needed, but one of the women in our church took it upon herself to decide how "hurt" Beth was and to attack me for it. Remember what I said about the sharks circling to devour the bleeding servant? Beth set her straight, but the incident plunged me into all those other fears. The cycle continued to spiral downward.

Ministry to Stage Two

If approached at just the right moment, and in just the right way, a Wounded Warrior at this stage of degeneration can still spill his hurt to another human being and receive ministry. More than anything else he needs simply to be listened to with a sympathetic ear. He doesn't usually want a solution, and un-asked-for advice may lead to rage and more withdrawal. He knows he wouldn't be able to pursue that advice with his fading energies, and so it only comes to him as more pressure to perform what he is losing his ability to perform. He just needs a safe place to dump the pain until he can recover his strength.

He can still look at roots and causes for his pain in terms of his own hidden sins, but he can do so only at times of his own choosing. Job's comforters were well-intentioned fools trying to convince him that his suffering was due to something for which he needed to repent. They were wrong. Unfortunately the Body of Christ today is full of Job's comforters. More than my share of them came to me in my pain to confront me "in love" and to show me that my plight was because of hidden sin. Hidden sin *was* present. It always is. But it wasn't the *cause* of my condition.

It may help a stage-two burn-out victim if you kidnap him from time to time and take him out for fun, but don't talk ministry when you do. During this period in my life, one man who didn't at that time attend our church would show up at my door from time to time and ask my wife, "Can Loren come out and play?" He might have a trailer full of go-carts waiting out front, or a movie he wanted to attend. Once it was motorcycles, which I don't ride well, but enjoyed anyway. Whatever he had up his sleeve, we'd play like kids for a few hours, without uttering a single word about church or ministry. It was healing and holy time from God, designed to restore my balance by rooting me in the good earth.

Intercede in prayer for your Wounded Warrior, but mostly at a distance where he doesn't have to respond. He'll feel it. Tell him you're praying, but don't tell him too much about what you're specifically asking God to do. He might take it as pressure to make your prayers happen.

Don't discuss his condition with others. If you do, he'll likely sense it and it will feed his paranoia. When you encounter others speaking about him in an unclean way, stop them. Don't even answer questions from those who are concerned, except to say that he can always use prayer from those who love him.

If the Lord gives you a specific Scripture reference or prophecy of hope for him, send it or give it in written form. It will feed his hope. Don't confront him face to face with it, but leave him free to read it and respond in private where he isn't responsible to you for his reaction.

Take up the sword on his behalf. If there is warfare in the church, he will treasure above all, your taking up his cause. I have treasured few gifts more than the one my elders gave me when we fought our last major battle as a church. We had changed our constitution to bring it more into conformity with the Scriptures. The reaction from a small minority was vicious and aimed at me personally. The objections were based on distortions of what we had enacted, and the opposition immediately turned to name-calling. I was accused of being everything from egomaniacal to cultish. In truth, I was on the edge of collapse after three years of warfare in which I had been mostly alone.

Every time the going got rough, my supporters and team members would lapse into paralysis and abandon the flock to be devoured by the wolves. This time the elders rallied and told me that it was their battle and not mine. That support was more healing to me than anyone could imagine. As a result, the church came through in shining triumph, and God began to fulfill what He had promised for us. At last I had gained a team of true co-workers.

Chapter 4

Stage 3 Wounding: Incapacity

4

Stage 3 Wounding: Incapacity

This is the most misunderstood of the three stages of wounding. As our team prepared for the seminar that gave birth to this book, we discussed roots and causes of wounding. We looked at performance orientation, the need for the wounded one to forgive those who betrayed him and actions that could be taken to facilitate recovery. We talked about praying through the hurts of betrayal until peace and resolution came. We examined changes in lifestyle and support systems. As we talked, I grew more and more angry, but didn't understand why at first.

I finally realized that what we were discussing was good medicine for someone in the earlier stages of wounding, but pure poison for the deeply wounded. The stage-three Wounded Warrior can no longer initiate or sustain his own recovery. Without some other sort of message mixed in, we would have driven a number of those present at the seminar into deeper hopelessness and despair because they would have come to the seminar in a state of *incapacity*. Had we gone no further in our discussions, we would have been asking them to do what they had lost the ability to do.

There are those so deeply wounded that they can only be carried, not exhorted. They need to be loved, not instructed. Many of them have already prayed through all the things listed above. It seems there's nothing left for them to try, and still they hemorrhage emotionally. They know by experience that there are no simple or quick means to the recovery they seek.

Part of this despair comes from the fact that the Body of Christ seldom is able to get beyond the demand for simplistic and quick fixes. Instantaneous miracles are what we have been trained to seek, especially in charismatic circles, which comprise a major share of my own beloved heritage. But there are no such miracles for the third-stage Wounded Warrior and he knows it. In fact, he's frightened by it and our simplistic solutions to his desperate problem serve only to drive him deeper into incapacity. Please give careful attention to this section, even if some of it offends some personally cherished theological point. I know what I'm talking about.

Physical Symptoms

A third-stage Wounded Warrior feels physically ill every day. He is so worn out, and his physical and spiritual resources so depleted, he feels like his spirit is installed in his body like a screw with the threads crossed. Physically, he feels slightly poisoned most of the time and suffers continual pain in various parts of his body. The constant flow of adrenalin produced by stress may have eroded the strength of his connective tissues and so there are aches and pains in joints and ligaments. My shoulders used to hurt so deeply in the connective tissues that no amount of over-the-counter pain killer brought relief. After a while my toe joints began to hurt and occasionally to spasm. I was having back problems and was seeing a chiropractor who complained that my ligaments were so weak that the adjustments he gave me wouldn't hold. Headaches became daily events, often arriving "on schedule" and with such intensity that I occasionally became nauseous. I would take three to five aspirins to ease the pain, only to begin shaking from the overdose of medicine. Lower dosages brought no relief. Painful fluid-filled blisters appeared on the balls of my feet that had nothing to do with physical overuse. They rose from well beneath the skin and were not athlete's foot. As I later recovered from my burn-out, the blisters disappeared.

Digestive disturbances become a daily experience and it seems that every meal leads to later pain. At this stage, food addictions and weaknesses are greatly aggravated. My craving for sugar increased at the same time that my physical ability to handle it vanished. For those who are stressed out, refined sugar is an absolute poison. I would compulsively ingest some sugar-laden delight and then be devastated at the effect produced in my body. No longer was there the sugar "high" followed by the low that normal people seem to experience. I went directly to the low, as if a toxin were running throughout my body. My eyes felt like they wanted to cross and I could barely stay awake. Sometimes sugar consumption brought on a headache.

Sleep is *never* satisfactory. Every night he may be tormented by difficulty falling asleep and every morning he wakes up feeling ill. People begin to comment on how bad he looks.

At this point the Wounded Warrior's heart may begin to act up by way of warning him that he must do something quickly to correct his physical and emotional condition. Angina and heart attacks are not uncommon among those predisposed to heart disease. I myself went to see the family doctor because my heart was missing beats and convulsing, sometimes with pain. After running a series of tests, he told me I was experiencing pre-ventricular contractions. In other words, sometimes the ventricles of my heart failed to pump in proper sequence. According to my doctor it wasn't a dangerous condition, but it was a clear warning. One young man I know began having false heart attacks. The pain in the chest and arm experienced by heart attack victims were both present, but his heart was healthy. Again, a warning.

Every other physical symptom listed under stage one and stage two is present, but in amplified form. Breakdown is imminent.

Emotional Condition

At this stage there is no respite from the sense that God has betrayed him. No divine promise can be relied upon because God has broken them all. There is no protection or help for him in the Lord. He has been utterly abandoned and even used by God without regard for his own personal needs. Although he may know (intellectually) that God loves him, there are almost no moments when he knows this with his heart. The betrayals seem devastatingly real.

For instance, in my daily devotions God would say to lengthen tent cords and enlarge the place of meeting because He was going to bring more growth in our church than we could house. The very next Sunday would be a record-low attendance for the year. God would promise me that my people would volunteer freely in the days of our power. There would be a workday on the church property scheduled for the following week and no one would show up.

I began to feel as if God were deliberately setting me up for disappointment just for torment's sake. I didn't want to hear anything from Him any more because my faith and trust were in tatters and each promise seemed like a set-up for more heartache. Today I see all those promises coming true for us, but during that period of time I'd lost my perspective.

Prayer life comes to a near standstill because there is nothing in it for the Wounded Warrior but pain. If he prays at all, he does so in settings where private intimacy with God is not possible. Ironically, he may continue to pray wonderfully in ministry situations because there he can still occasionally feel the anointing and the presence of God, but often feels betrayed afterward because the Lord doesn't seem to be there for him personally.

The wounded one has no protection against the blows and pressures of daily life. Every breakdown of routine, every failure of others to carry out their tasks as they overlap with his, occasions the deepest depression or even rage. Several times I stopped assigning tasks to others because I could no longer deal with the devastation that came from feeling personally let down when the tasks weren't performed. I could no longer risk my helpers failing me.

No resiliency remains, either emotionally or physically. Any exertion becomes extremely painful for every part of body and spirit. The Wounded Warrior in stage three of degeneration feels like a fighter who can no longer ward off his opponent's blows. He can't even hold up his fists any more. All he can do is resolve to remain in the ring and take it. Had the blows come with enough space between them, he could have recovered and remained on top of things, but too many pressures, crises and betrayals have piled one on top of another. There has been no breathing room, and now he is broken.

For the first time in my life I was driven to active hatred. With no time to think and pray through the hurts, pressures and betrayals as they came at me, I felt myself backed into a corner until I had nothing left but rage. The group of persecutors was small, but effective, and the more so because of my fatigue. For my love they had returned criticism. For my best counsel they had returned distorted reflections of all I had said, and, to make matters worse, they had enlisted others in the attack. They would say, "He doesn't love us," while I stumbled around exhausted from being there for them in their emergencies day after day in counsel, often into the wee hours of the morning. The darkness and confusion they generated penetrated even the beauty of our worship. Scarcely had the echoes of one incident died out before I'd find myself facing another. My spirituality was stripped bare and I was left with raw emotion over which I had little or no control.

The Wounded Warrior's every nerve is afire. Unless extraordinarily good restraints were built into the character of the wounded one early in his life, then one who has otherwise been kind and loving may suddenly become explosive in his anger. Even violent. Spouses of such wounded ones may be confused and hurt by violent reactions to what seem to be small requests or insignificant irritants. The wounded one is literally screaming inside with rage and desperation. Gone are the physical resources that enable the mind to fight off craziness.

I believe, but cannot substantiate, that there are certain physical resources, chemicals or nutrients stored or produced by the body and then utilized to combat stress. They enable us to maintain a grip on reality when reality becomes painful. Under certain conditions of prolonged stress these resources are exhausted and the body has a most difficult time replacing them. Medical science provides very little help at this point because there seems to be no method for measuring what these resources are or how to renew them. The family doctor can only declare that his tests reveal no measurable physical abnormalities. It's frustrating, because the sufferer knows what pain he's in and he also knows he is not a hypochondriac.

When we fought the last major battle in our church that I mentioned in the previous chapter, I was caught off guard by my reaction. I had been feeling pretty good because the church had been at peace for some time. I believed I had recovered from the devastation of betrayals from friends and loved ones, betrayals I had suffered in the first couple of years after we opened the church. What I had not expected was that a number of my family members (not my wife), most of whom were members of the church, abandoned me—or seemed to do so—in my hour of need. Some even led the opposition.

The abandonment lasted only a week or so

before most understood and took up my cause, but the damage was already done. None of those resources I just mentioned were there for me to draw upon. It was as if a great black hole opened up beneath me and was sucking me downward with a muddy, swirling motion. I remember thinking what a relief it would be just to let go and go completely crazy. My mother-in-law, who lives with us and who has experienced two nervous breakdowns of her own, heard my symptoms and went ashen-white. She knew what was happening. I took a vacation and demanded that I not be seen or contacted by anyone until I returned. Once gone, I was able to hold my own for a week or two, but then the depression worsened and I felt my world was coming to an end. In the midst of it all, elder Jim Tiffany heard the call of the Spirit and he and his wife, Marcia, took Beth and me out to a movie and for coffee afterwards. It was the right moment. My grip on reality was restored as he spoke positive truth to me concerning the condition of our church and the effectiveness of my ministry. I began to recover.

The servant who has reached this stage of wounding suffers almost uncontrollable paranoia. He finds himself afraid in relation to almost every aspect of his ministry. Offerings will be inadequate; the church will lose members; longstanding and powerful leaders will leave; and on and on. Who will betray him next? Who is talking? From past experience he knows no one will stand with him and He begins to picture conflict situations in which he walks out or resigns. He mentally rehearses blistering speeches he wishes he could make in response to hurtful situations.

His inability to receive love worsens. He's so bruised that even the embrace of a safe family member causes pain. Emotional withdrawal is now nearly constant and moments of vulnerability are most rare. I'm still learning to kiss my wife again. In the depth of my wounding I couldn't stand to have anything or anyone "in my face," demanding a response. The simple offer of frontal affection at first irritated me and then ignited rage if my barriers weren't respected.

Ministry during this stage is enormously painful. I can recall counseling sessions in which I cried out in mortal desperation to God, "Please! Make it stop!!" as some troubled complainer droned on. The wounded one has nothing left to give. Every sermon, every teaching, every bit of counsel given requires gargantuan efforts on his part.

Taking an extended vacation may help, but often only serves to make matters worse, as it did for me. In some cases, the wounded one may be so filled with anxiety concerning what might be going wrong at home that limited doses of contact with work may be necessary to keep him in touch with reality.

Resistance to all sorts of addictive behavior is impaired at this stage. I worry that many Wounded Warriors may be getting chemical help from their personal physicians at a time when dependency is a real danger. Drugs only suppress the problem, rather than solve it, and there will be a debt to pay later. My personal physician and I agreed that even so innocent a drug as a sleeping pill would have been dangerous for me, and so I resolved not to use them. I found myself retreating into video games. I was addicted to them, but they didn't relieve my stress. Anyone who has played them knows they're a very tense way to have fun. I know one Wounded Warrior who becomes obsessed with television. Yet another is a rude and idolatrous fanatic about television football. There are as many choices as there are people.

Continually suppressed emotions come back in perverted form and the Wounded Warrior has probably long been inadequately dealing with his feelings. I felt I had been *forced* to suppress mine. If I shared what I really felt with anyone other than my wife—or with the elders later on—the shock waves in the fellowship were more trouble than the relief was worth. Our society is so sick about authority that any leader who shares a weakness or a sin too openly, or in the wrong company, will certainly pay for it later. The spirit of our society is to look for faults in leadership and to use them to tear down and to weaken the leader's effectiveness. When we can't find a legitimate flaw, we just invent one. The wolves use weakness as a pretext to attack and accuse while the weak and insecure use it as an excuse to spread poison among others who are weak. All of it adds to the stress, and so the downward slide of the Wounded Warrior accelerates. I can remember thinking bitterly that because of the ministry, I had neither the right nor the time to feel.

Under normal conditions, morality is a gift for a strong man of God. Temptations come as they always do, but are routinely bested. In the deeply Wounded Warrior, however, critical strengths have been catastrophically eroded so that whatever cracks remain in his inner being, whatever areas of the flesh or of sin that God has not been allowed to transform, may become gaping chasms under pressure. By natural strength and spiritual integrity he's controlled his sin nature in the past, but his capacity to control is now gone.

Therefore, the third-stage Wounded Warrior may find himself compulsively violating what he knows to be biblical moral imperatives. The following are confessions I've heard in counseling. He may be irresistibly drawn to pornography and be driven deeper into wounding by the stress produced by the guilt over his attraction. He may find himself compulsively masturbating as a way of relieving pressures. He may begin to think unexplainably violent thoughts and to visualize himself doing violent things. He may find himself drawn to women other than his wife. He may begin to drink excessively in private. He may begin to drive too fast too much of the time. This list could go on and on. All of it adds to his guilt burden. He can't understand the loss of control that has led him to do these things. Guilt over the loss of control produces more stress which drives him deeper into incapacity.

His confidence in his anointing and in his ability to minister may be utterly destroyed and he may even question his calling. This is largely due to a loss of perspective. In his weakened condition he can focus only on small things, rather than the whole picture. Immediate problems seem eternal, when, under normal conditions, he would be able to see them as temporary. In seems to him that his best efforts and most costly expenditures of energy have not produced the fruit he needs to sustain himself. He has given the best he has to offer and has received scorn and criticism in return. If he counsels, he may have forgotten that people take years to change, rather than days or months. He sees every setback suffered by a counselee as his personal failure. He may talk of leaving his ministry and may even hint at suicide. Take this threat seriously in most cases and do what you can to protect him from himself. Better to be wrong and safe than wrong and wishing you'd listened. Usually such talk is just catharsis, noise to be heard and ignored, but you can never be certain.

Ministry to Stage Three

Don't be a "Job's comforter." Avoid confronting the wounded one with bitter-root judgments or sin that may have created his problem. At this stage he is in no condition at all to do that kind of introspection or to deal with the healing process associated with it. There are no resources left in him to do so. He has already crucified himself with self-examination and has come up empty. He's probably repented in every way he knows how and, like Job, he may know by now that the suffering under which he labors is not the result of his sin. But whether it is or is not the fruit of sin in his life, this is not the time for corrective ministry. "Nouthetic" (confrontive) counseling may drive him over the edge. Corrective ministry is possibly only *after* some recovery of strength. Don't analyze the roots of the problem unless he asks for analysis and then do so only sparingly.

In most cases, deliverance ministry is a foolish approach. Spirits of oppression are not the source of his problem. He will not get better as a result of your prayers for deliverance and will only feel more betrayed by God for his failure to improve. Spirits may be contributing to the problem, but they are not the root of it. If you must cast demons off of, or out of him, do so where he cannot hear.

It sounds strange, but it may cause more harm than good to tell the Wounded Warrior that God loves him. He can't believe that God loves him and is convinced that the evidence points to the absence of that love. Your affirmation of it only brings him face to face with his pain. Tell him that *you* love him. He may not believe it, but it's more tangible than the love of a God he can neither see nor any longer feel. It will then be your responsibility to prove that you mean what you say by not failing him or betraying him.

Don't tell the third-stage sufferer what inner imperfections God is burning out of his nature, or that this is a sanctifying, purifying experience sent or used by God to "get the 'gunk' out." It may be true that God is, in fact, using the situation to accomplish just such a cleansing, but to the wounded one God is a betrayer and he has had enough of pain. Besides, he already instinctively knows that what you're saying is true. If he didn't, he'd be long gone already.

Respect his fences and his withdrawal. Be secure enough not to take them as personal rejection. He simply can no longer respond normally to others and, if he is pushed to do so, the result may be an explosion of rage, followed by a deeper flight from relationships. Don't demand that he talk to you or that he listen to your advice. Let him choose the sharing times.

Don't talk to him about time management. This is seldom, if ever, the problem. Management of time is just another thing to do, and he can't face any more things to do. Don't tell him he needs to delegate more of his work. He's been let down too often by those who didn't follow through on their tasks and can no longer risk being wounded in that area.

Don't tell him to praise God *for* all things (Eph. 5:20). This is wonderful scriptural counsel to give to a healthy sufferer, but is a cruel burden to place on an incapacitated Wounded Warrior. He *can't* do it. His best approach to God is an honest cry of rage. All I had left at this stage was my honesty about how I felt. That's how I knew I still had a relationship with God. I called Him every name in the book, both fair and foul, and He was big enough not to be offended by it as I got it off my chest. Better to have an angry relationship in which communication still goes on than to have no relationship at all.

As with stage-two Wounded Warriors, don't deliver face-to-face prophecies that *must* be responded to, no matter how encouraging their content may be. That's sandpaper on open scabs. Write it out and send it by mail or deliver it by hand with the understanding that it can be read later, privately.

The best praying for a stage-three Wounded Warrior is done at a respectful distance. Don't tell your wounded one what you're praying for because that makes him responsible to do something about it. Just let him know you're praying and that you care. Let it stop there. He'll be able to take encouragement from such assurance without feeling any pressure to respond.

Love him in ways that demand no response. Whether you are family or friend, don't "get in his face" with frontal hugs and penetrating eye contact. Many wounded ones absolutely cannot stand the intensity of full frontal interaction so let hugs be sideways or from behind and don't demand eye contact. Let expressions of love take the form of a touch on the hand or an affectionate poke in the ribs.

Listen. Be available. The rare moment of vulnerability may surface at any time. I used to awaken Beth in bed, late at night, usually rousing her from a sound sleep. I couldn't help it. That's when I was able to spill my pain, and I knew that if I let the moment go, I'd not be able to manufacture it later. Beth understood more than anyone else that I didn't want answers to my sharing, that it was enough for me just to be able to express myself to one who wouldn't be dragged down by my gloomy outlook.

Believe in your Wounded Warrior, and tell him about it. Beth used to assure me over and over again that I was a good pastor and father, because I was no longer certain I was a good anything. See and affirm the wounded one's gifts and don't waver in your faith for him.

Send encouraging gifts and cards of love and appreciation for what the wounded one has given to you, but remember not to demand any sort of response.

At the appropriate time, pursue the wounded one and speak truth to him about what's right and good in the ministry and in his life. Time this carefully in the Spirit, because, if approached at the wrong time, the wounded one can be driven farther into withdrawal. A good illustration is the story I told earlier about one of the elders who came to me at the bottom of my despair and spoke truth to me again. The Wounded Warrior is in danger of completely losing his grip on reality. While withdrawal is needed as a tool for healing, it can also be a prison in which there are no correctives against a fatal loss of perspective. Without those correctives, the nightmare of despair can become both bottomless and endless.

Chapter 5

Personal Survival: What the Wounded One Can Do

5

Personal Survival: What the Wounded One Can Do

At the seminar on the Wounded Warrior we taught in Spokane, Washington, someone asked how I survived my own wounding. There are many facets to my answer. I have a wife who instinctively did for me what needed to be done. At a crucial point I had a friend who tracked me down and spoke edifying truth to me. There were a few whom the Lord quickened to send me encouragement in the mail or to deliver written prophecies by hand. But by and large, most people did all the wrong things.

The most important thing that enabled me to survive was the gift of mental discipline bestowed on me by God's grace somewhere in the course of my life. Part of it was the training I received as a child when I was not allowed to express my emotions in ways destructive to others. That training formed a second nature restraint that I could rely on without having to work at it. I was given a good foundation in both affection and discipline so that, in the midst of the most severe tests, I have been able to know what I know well enough to survive.

I realize many of us weren't given this training as children. Without it the battle for control is immeasurably more difficult, but still winnable. I know one young minister in the depths of wounding who became abusive with his wife and son for a time. He simply lost control. The walls of restraint hadn't been provided in his early life and he broke under the pressure of the crisis he faced. Early in his wounding, the discipline of prayer and of his Christian walk kept him kind and gentle, but he was horrified at what came out of him later. He exploded and then fought for discipline with all his failing strength. He struggled. He wept. He despaired. He even considered divorcing his wife. He pled for the Lord's discipline and sought wise and compassionate counsel. In the end the Lord provided for him the discipline he lacked and God became Father to him. So— it's more difficult, but it's possible. The war can be won.

Even at the depth of my own wounding I disciplined myself to weigh the consequences of losing control against the pain of hanging on, and therefore refused to surrender to insanity. I knew that every time I acted on my anger, I would only create more stress for myself than I was already suffering. I knew most people could never understand and would only be hurt by my outbursts. Matters would be worse in the end. If I turned to accusation as means of alleviating my inner pressure, I would only drive people to defend themselves by attacking me.

I knew that if I couldn't make it work at Cornerstone, there was no place else for me to go. My integrity would forever be in question, even in my own eyes.

I was also able to take into account what my children would lose if I caved in. Because I knew that the pain I would suffer for taking their heritage from them was worse than the pain I was already experiencing, I hung on. The first principle of survival is, therefore, to know what you know for your own sake and for the sake of others who depend on you. You won't always succeed, but the effort may enable you to survive.

During this time I learned that feelings simply exist. In and of themselves, they are morally neutral. As an extension of our sinful flesh, they are at least forgivable. There is a certain sense in which we are helpless to control those feelings that don't line up with God's nature, so that our only hope is to confess our helplessness and receive the Lord's mercy. Feelings don't necessarily have substance, nor do they necessarily reflect reality. And they are profoundly poor determiners of what I should do in the real world.

I survived, in part, by learning to separate what I felt from what I did. I learned that what is right to do, or true to believe, often has little or nothing to do with what I feel. I can have a feeling in one part of myself and do the opposite of that feeling in another part of myself just because the doing of the thing is objectively right. Unfortunately, most of us stumble through life acting out our subjectivities, living as victims of our emotions and consistently reaping trouble for it.

> The heart is more deceitful than all else And is desperately sick; Who can understand it? (Jer. 17:9)

Living from feelings is fine when feelings coincide with reality or with what is objectively right, but every one of us must somehow learn to do what is objectively right, even when our emotions conflict with this approach. Know what you know, and insofar as your incapacity at the depth of your wounding will allow it, *do* what you know. You may not succeed. You may be too "wasted" in your energies to succeed. But the effort may keep you sane and you will learn an inner discipline that yields huge dividends later.

The second principle of survival is to "embrace the fireball." I got the phrase from a dream that a young man once asked me to interpret. In the dream the Lord Jesus appeared to him and presented him with a ball of fire about the size of a basketball. He was instructed to hug it to himself. When he obeyed, the pain was excruciating, and yet there was something terribly good about it. I knew the Lord was about to plunge him into suffering and that he was to embrace it for its cleasing effect, rather than fight it.

> Beloved, do not be surprised at the fiery ordeal among you, which comes upon you for your test-

ing, as though some strange thing were happening to you; But to the degree that you share the sufferings of Christ, keep on rejoicing; so that also at the revelation of His glory, you may rejoice with exultation. (1 Pet. 4:12-13)

Therefore since Christ has suffered in the flesh, arm yourselves also with the same purpose, because he who has suffered in the flesh has ceased from sin,... (1 Pet. 4:1)

Although I couldn't tolerate others telling me that my experience was for sanctification, I knew within myself that it was. I even knew it was for no specific wrongdoing. I have a task to perform for the Lord, and for that task my personality, gifts, abilities and even my way of meeting life must be honed, refined and changed.

There were times when I lost touch with this basic knowledge, but on the whole it contributed to my continuing sanity. I learned that the difference between redemptive suffering and destructive misery is the degree to which one fights, rather that accepts, the pain. I found peace in the embracing of it. I wasn't constant in that peace, but I did survive and I was certainly changed.

"Though He slay me, I will hope in Him" (Job 13:15). Job went on to protest his innocence and did, in fact, carry on a lengthy argument with God. But at the end, when the Lord revealed himself, Job was compelled to admit, "I have heard of Thee by the hearing of the ear; But now my eye sees Thee; Therefore I retract, And I repent in dust and ashes" (Job 42:5-6). Job didn't and couldn't describe what it was he'd learned. I myself can't really tell you what's different about me today, but people who've known me through the years notice it. I'm better listened to now than I was five years ago.

Although my wounds have healed, I still keep a piece of that pain in my heart. It's a source of balance and of sober joy to me and, without it, I have no wisdom. One of the most important lessons I've learned is that knowledge comes from study, but wisdom comes from pain. I, therefore, welcome the pain and have developed a new understanding of what the Preacher meant when he wrote:

> Sorrow is better than laughter, For when a face is sad a heart may be happy. The mind of the wise is in the house of mourning, While the mind of fools is in the house of pleasure. (Eccles. 7:3-4)

Learn to love obedience for obedience's sake. I used to love to serve the Lord because I loved the fruit I saw in my ministry. It was fun to produce for Him. Part of my suffering was that God took away my ability to produce by sending me a gang of locusts to eat it all up. I had to learn to obey, whether I saw fruit or not. It had to become enough for me emotionally just to know that I had done that which God had asked me to do. I began to teach others that obedience to the Lord must be its own reward. The doing of ministry, and not the fruit of doing ministry, must ever be my joy.

Find a safe environment in which regularly to

dump what you feel, and do the dumping as an act of obedience to God. It may not be easy, but it is certainly necessary. James 5:16 is much neglected among Protestants today and especially among clergy, "Therefore, confess your sins to one another, and pray for one another, so that you may be healed."

For me it was our elders' group that meets weekly as a fellowship with our wives. These men and women are partners with me in ministry and we've developed a trust relationship in spite of the many ways in which we have failed one another. For a time I made it a discipline to report to them weekly on my emotional state. They needed to know, and I needed to objectify what I felt by sharing it. There were times when I wanted to hide, but I worked against the impulse because I knew it spelled the difference between recovery and failure.

Learn Not To Share With Wounders

Multitudes of well-intentioned church people are ready to show deepest concern and love for you and your condition. Not all are safe. "I would never hurt you," they promise, "Please tell me if I ever do." These people appear in many forms and may be of either gender.

I'll tell you my own story and you can adapt it to your situation. It's actually a composite of many stories, rather than just one, since there are people I'd like to protect.

Unfortunately, most of the wounders who have crossed my path have been broken women with a need to gain some kind of control over authority figures in their lives. Obviously this kind of problem isn't limited to women, but women seem more susceptible to it. I'm sorry I must say this and I realize I may take some abuse for it in this increasingly feminist society, but it's true. This sort of woman "gentles" her way into the life of a male leader in trouble, until, in some weak moment when he's feeling leaky, she gets him to spill a portion of his pain.

Because these women run in "packs," a whole group of them are soon sharing this grave "concern" and praying up a storm, fanning the flames of their emotions and becoming more and more deluded. They don't believe they're speaking in any unrighteous way because, after all, these women with whom they share are their freinds and they are just submitting their burdens and perceptions to trusted others for confirmation and balance. They may share these burdens with their husbands as well, and if the man isn't exceptionally strong he may be drawn into the delusion and the talk.

Before long, the group has arrived at a solution for, or an analysis of, the leader's problem and they want to minister to it. The solution, and/ or analysis, is usually way off the mark and often comes as a set of accusations, spoken "in love," but which cut the wounded one to the heart.

Then, when he rejects their "prophetic word" because of its inaccuracy, he is seen as one who doesn't listen and cannot receive correction.

Understand that these are well-intentioned saints of the Lord, acting with no awareness of what it is they're really doing. Love them, but avoid sharing with them anything of substance from your own heart.

I know of no better way to identify wounders and to avoid falling into their traps than to listen to your mate. Beth is a whole woman who has unfailingly spotted such hidden reefs and warned me ahead of time. I had to learn the hard way that she was right by suffering the situation I described above on a couple of occasions. Today I listen.

If you're a Wounded Warrior, and you're not married, or if your spouse doesn't have this type of perception, or is wounded herself (or himself), then seek out reliable prophets in your flock who can warn you concerning impending doom and who can see the sin in the hearts of people. Then heed them for your own sake and for the sake of the fellowship you lead.

Feed your weakened spirit in ways that don't require energy expenditures. First, cleanse your mind of standard Christian pietistic ideas of how to get refreshment from the Lord, and then prepare yourself for something that may be different for you. Standard Christian piety is fine under normal conditions, but it presents demands that can no longer be met by many deeply wounded ones. In

His grace, God can refresh, instruct and correct His servants from a multitude of unlikely sources. Remember that He spoke to Balaam by the mouth of an ass.

Try listening to good music, both secular and sacred. At one point in the process of my recovery I got out some old Joni Mitchell records from my "hippie" days. Her poetry was marvelous and her music deeply melancholy, with an ever-present reminder of a simpler life. Sometimes she sang in such a beautiful way of such dismal hopelessness that if the music weren't so good, the listener would be crushed. It expressed something of what was inside of me and, by expressing it, released it. I sat before the stereo and cried on several occasions.

I went to movies like the "Rocky" series in which a nobody from a Philadelphia slum fought his way to the top, was beaten and then fought his way back again. The "Star Trek" and "Star Wars" series both got to me. Both were about people who snatched victory from the jaws of defeat, who came from behind to overcome powerful enemies.

I reread J.R.R. Tolkien's *The Lord of the Rings* and a whole group of other fantasies. I needed a fresh injection of imagination and magic in my life in order to renew my sense of the supernatural and God gave it to me in some of the world's great literature.

All of these books and movies were important to me because the theme common to all of them is recovery of power after a crushing defeat. They tell of little men doing great things in the face of terrible odds. They include lessons on the misuse of power and on the power to be found in weakness. They reminded me that I'm a winner by nature and by anointing, I hadn't lost the war, but the cost of winning had left me so defeated and broken that I had forgotten what strength felt like.

These simple movies and wonderful books rekindled a dying flame and sent me soaring. To date, I've read Tolkien five times and have seen each of the "Rocky" movies, and each of the space movies, more times than I care to admit. God used those secular sources to revitalize the reading of His Word for me and, as a result, I saw things in the Scriptures I hadn't seen before. The Bible had new encouragement in it as God refreshed me from some unlikely springs.

Others might find renewal in the stories of Robin Hood or King Arthur. Still others might be drawn to great classical music or to poetry. Time spent in the vastness of nature might recall greatness and so bring restoration. Jesus Himself went to the mountaintop to pray.

In short, nourish your spirit on great music, great poetry, heroic stories and films, or whatever else rekindles your dying flame. And don't limit the kinds of vehicles God can use to do that. All true beauty and truth come from Him. Whatever you consume, let it stand under the judgment of the eternal Word, the Bible. Chew the meat and spit out the bones.

Get someone to cover for you. In the beginning I told you I might upset your theology, didn't I? What I mean is that you need to establish some protection for yourself that you are not personally responsible for maintaining. My wife and my mother-in-law (who lives with us) do this for me. When they see that my energies are expended, they keep people away.

My wife is clever enough to tell selective truths about my availability. She doesn't lie. She tells you only what you really must know so that you hang up the phone understanding that I cannot be reached. My mother-in-law doesn't think so quickly as my wife does and is, therefore, prone to tell you I'm not at home, when, in fact, I am. My office secretary takes a similar approach.

The point is that there are times when I'm not the one to decide when I've spent too much of myself. I'm not good at saying no to people. I don't have Beth's and her mother's wisdom in that area and so I let them protect me.

If you're still not convinced, I'll give you some examples of "sanctified lying." In Joshua 2, Rahab the harlot lied to protect the spies sent from Joshua to spy out Jericho. In Judges 4, Jael deceived Sisera in order to kill him for the sake of the people of Israel. 'Nuff said?

Don't assume that the cause of your wounding is some personal sin or character flaw. Job suffered terribly, but not as a result of any personal shortcoming. Although his suffering was not the result of unrighteousness on his part, he was changed by the experience and his personal relationship with God was transformed. The same transformation will be yours if you but wait it out.

When you can't praise God, be honest. Call Him names. He'll probably fall off His throne laughing. Suppression brings reaping, while honesty cleanses. In my deepest rage and despair I even swore at Him. I discovered He doesn't have virgin ears and that His presence is the one completely safe place in all the world in which I can be whatever I happen to be at the moment. Better to hurl my rage and accusation at God than not to pray at all. You won't have to read far in the Psalms to find that there is scriptural precedent for what I'm saying.

If the obstacles you face in your situation seem too big to beat, at least don't quit. The fact that you don't quit will itself win the day for you. The great spiritual warfare passage (in Eph. 6), places great emphasis on "standing firm." You aren't required to conquer or take land or even function at full capacity. You have only to refuse to move for the victory to be assured.

First, by your refusal to move, you give God room to work the sort of transformation in your heart that He made in Job's heart. Often those who flee the scene of the pain only remove themselves from the fire God set to test them, and they cheat themselves of the strength and wisdom that develop only in the heat of tribulation and death.

Second, in your standing firm you break the heart of your enemy, whether that enemy is a spiritual force, a stituation or a person. I once told a troublemaker, "I'm tougher than anyone here and I'll be here long after you're gone." Her whole crowd is now history, while I reap an abundant harvest. God is prospering the ministry. You may be so broken you can no longer fight, but you can at least refuse to get out of the ring.

Know your innocence. Often your wounding is the result of a barrage of accusations from those to whom you minister and for whom you've poured forth your best gifts of love. Because you know you've made mistakes, your tendency may be to try to wear what they are saying about you. Somehow you feel that if you could just do everything right, everyone would love you for it.

This is, of course, a foolish hope. There comes a time when you must call a halt to self-examination and introspection and take stock of your integrity. Claim your innocence. There came a time when I finally had to say, "I have not done that of which you accuse me. I have not manipulated. I never said what you accuse me of having said. I didn't mean what you insist I meant when I said thus-and-such. My ambition is for the Lord and not for personal gain as you insinuate. I did not betray to others what you shared in confidence. It was you, yourself, who leaked the information and someone else who talked about it."

I think you get the idea. I wasn't perfect, but I had not sinned against these people. I had to be driven to the point of rage before I could take this stand. I had nearly destroyed myself with misplaced guilt, doubts and questions by the time I got there, but it was a tremendous relief when I finally arrived at this point.

Those of us with pastor's hearts have a very difficult time facing the fact that people are basically nasty. We want to believe in people, and we'd rather blame ourselves than face the possibility that the heart of a loved one might be as black as night.

Get mad. Pray the "bloody" Psalms. God will know what to do with them, even if, in your rage, you intend more than is righteous. In this praying, you will find a holy way to experience catharsis, while spiritual power is released to defeat your enemies. Please put away any theological problems with this advice, and simply do what the Scriptures do. Here are some quotes:

> Contend, O Lord, with those who contend with me; Fight against those who fight against me. Take hold of buckler and shield, And rise up for my help. Draw also the spear and the battle-ax to meet those who pursue me; ...Let those be ashamed and dishonored who seek my life; Let those be turned back and humiliated who devise evil against me... Let their way be dark and slippery, With the angel of the Lord pursuing them... Let destruction come upon him unawares; And let the net which he hid catch him-

self; Into that very destruction let him fall. (Ps. 35:1-8)

O God, shatter their teeth in their mouth; Break out the fangs of the young lions, O Lord. Let them flow away like water that runs off; When he aims his arrows, let them be as headless shafts. (Ps. 58:6-7)

Save me, O God, For the waters have come up to my soul. I have sunk in deep mire, and there is no foothold; I have come into deep waters, and the flood overflows me. I am weary with my crying; my throat is parched; My eyes fail while I wait for my God. Those who hate me without cause are more than the hairs of my head; Those who would destroy me are powerful. What I did not steal, I then have to restore.... for Thy sake I have borne reproach; Dishonor has covered my face. I have become estranged from my brothers, And an alien to my mother's sons.... Reproach has broken my heart, and I am so sick. And I looked for sympathy, but there was none, And for comforters, but I found none. They also gave me gall for my food, And for my thirst they gave me vinegar to drink. May their table before them become a snare; And when they are at peace, may it become a trap. May their eyes grow dim so that they cannot see, And may their loins shake continually. Pour out Thine indignation on them, And may Thy burning anger overtake them. May their camp be desolate; May none dwell in their tents.... May they be blotted out of the book of life, And may they not be recorded with the righteous. (Ps. 69)

O God of my praise, Do not be silent! For they have opened the wicked and deceitful mouth against me; They have spoken against me with a lying tongue. They have also surrounded me with words of hatred, And fought against me without cause. In return for my love they act as my accusers; But I am in prayer. Thus they have repaid me evil for good, And hatred for my love. Appoint a wicked man over him; And let an accuser stand at his right hand. When he is judged, let him come forth guilty; And let his prayer become sin. Let his days be few; Let another take his office. Let his children wander about and beg; And let them seek sustenance far from their ruined homes. Let the creditor seize all that he has; And let the stranger plunder the product of his labor. Let there be none to extend lovingkindness to him, Nor any to be gracious to his fatherless children. Let his posterity be cut off; In a following generation let their name be blotted out. (Ps. 109:1-13)

In the end, each of those who falsely accused and persecuted me was shamed before the congregation. While I did next to nothing, God sovereignly revealed their sin before the whole flock until with one voice the fellowship cried, "Enough!"

When the judgment of God falls on such people, it is redemptive, but when they reap the Law, full-grown, the end is devastation. The judgment of God restores the repentant heart while the reaping of the Law simply destroys. "God is not mocked; for whatever a man sows, this he will also reap" (Gal. 6.7). Therefore, in the mystery of God, such bloody prayers are really prayers for mercy.

The tragedy in our case was that most of those who did these things to me were never able to repent. As I followed the histories of these people after they left us, I discovered a consistent pattern of disaster. There were bankruptcies, incest, family break-ups and fires, to name but a few. It is a fearsome thing to fall into the hands of the living God.

Yet, if any one of these people came to my door needing help, I'd give it. One or two of them wouldn't be allowed back into the flock without some real repentance and change, but all would be welcome to my personal ministry.

Chapter 6

Breaking Destructive
Life Patterns

6

Breaking Destructive Life Patterns

Wounded Warriors are often captives to what they do, sacrificing self and health beyond the true call of God. I remember thinking—and rightly so—that my life and faith should be a model for others. The next thought was always, "But where is my joy? Would I invite others into this pain I'm in? Is the Christian walk an invitation to fatigue? Do I really want others to be as unbalanced as I am?" Because of the questions, recovering from my wounding and finding my joy again became issues of personal integrity. How could I preach the peace of God when I had so little of it myself? In describing patterns that need breaking I've tried not to duplicate things already covered in previous chapters except where emphasis is needed.

The Personal Obligation Pattern

Most Wounded Warriors feel obligated to everyone. Sometimes the problem is a fear of not being liked or loved for saying no once in a while.

Or the Wounded Warrior may genuinely feel that without him terrible things will happen in the lives of those who look to him for ministry. He sees their failures as his own failures and therefore can't risk letting them fail. The point is that he can't withdraw from perceived obligations often enough to remain healthy. He is so locked-in that sometimes he won't even permit others to say no on his behalf.

I learned to say no by becoming angry enough with people and with my condition that I was driven to action. I'm still not good at it, but I've made a healthy beginning. For instance, the telephone rings and it's Melvin calling again with the same story he tells again and again, with the same pain, again and again and again. I'm not home, but my wife promises I'll return his call. I don't. Angrily I don't. Feels good, too. And Melvin survives. Wonder of wonders!

The building committee is meeting on my day off. They'll make decisions concerning the shape of our new building that I'll hate later. My pastoral perspective is needed. The chairman knew better than to schedule it for that day, darn his hide! Well, I'm not going! Take that! Talked to the architect two days later. Corrected some errors. Everybody lived.

Planning our vacation. Gosh, I need it this year! But we're supposed to be with family. Aunt Maimie will be there. She's been judging me for fifteen years and she'll be at it again. She won't say anything to me directly, but I'll feel it and her husband will hear about it later. Can't handle that this year. I need this vacation away from the stress of juggling other people's feelings and I won't get it with her there. I refuse to deal with that situation again this year! The family will be upset if we don't come? Good! I won't be there to see it! Now where's another place we can go and be alone?

The Self-Sacrificing Pattern

My family has an inherited disease. My minister father has it. My brothers and sisters have it. I have it. It's an attitude that goes something like this: "If I'm not working to exhaustion, I'm not working hard enough." Fun is a waste of precious ministry time. Therefore, time for fun means time for guilt. Exercise is time taken away from work time. More guilt. Then guilt for not exercising. Even sleep is a distraction from the task of ministry. Hobbies are out. They're for the uncommitted who have time for such empty pursuits. The answer to this one is so obvious I shouldn't even have to spell it out.

Here are some solutions I found for myself. Three years ago Beth and I bought a week at a time-share condominium. We couldn't afford it, but we knew we needed it. For that week each year, we leave our kids with their grandmother while the two of us spend a week alone together in shameless self-indulgence. And God has approved so heartily that He's enabled us to pay for it! I don't know what it will take for you, but find some way to cultivate a little "holy selfishness."

Concerning the issue of *my* time, God spoke to me directly. Twice. One afternoon in the depth of my wounding when I was too tired to work (but hadn't the courage to leave the office and actually *look* like I wasn't working) God said simply, *"Instead of feeling guilty for these stolen moments, why not thank Me for the opportunity to rest?"* Obediently, I began a simple but refreshing discipline of doing just that. Try it. You'll like it. You'll feel like a kid stealing candy for a while, but you'll like it just the same and it may save your sanity.

There is, of course, the simple principle that "all work and no play makes Jack a dull boy." Play time is holy time. I used to feel guilty for taking time out with the one I mentioned earlier who would come over to my house and jokingly ask my wife if I could come out and play. A good laugh serves at least as well as twenty minutes in prayer for the release of tension and the refreshment of the soul. "A joyful heart is good medicine, But a broken spirit dries up the bones" (Prov. 17:22). Take time for some things you enjoy, and hang the guilt.

The second time He spoke He said, *"If you don't start exercising, you're going to die."* I knew I wasn't in imminent danger of losing my life, but I was in imminent danger of losing something I wouldn't be able to recover. Perhaps it's an echo of my Osage Indian heritage on my father's side, but my personal makeup is such that strength is

important to me—both physical and spiritual.
Strength has been one of God's best natural gifts
to me. I know, too, that ever since God formed
man from dust and breathed his personal spirit
into him, body and spirit have been interdepen-
dent. Physical health profoundly affects spiritual
health and vice versa. I was becoming desperately
weak and sick in my body because of the stress in
my life, and it was affecting me spiritually as well.

So deeply burned out and emotionally
wounded was I that I couldn't find the strength to
begin an exercise program on my own initiative,
despite the Lord's warning. But I've learned that
when I'm unable to obey the Lord freely, He'll set
up a situation in which I am compelled to do so.
Not that He violates my free will. It's just that I
gave Him blanket permission long ago to do with
me as He would, and I've not yet withdrawn it.
My father (the earthly one) began to notice the de-
terioration in my health and purchased a member-
ship for me in a local athletic club. Because he had
spent money, my personal-obligation pattern
clicked in—beneficially for once—and I began to
exercise. I chose body building because that's
what I enjoy. For you, it might be racquet ball or
jogging or swimming. The point is that exercise is
critical to the recovery of any Wounded Warrior.

I now spend eight hours each week pumping
iron at a local gym. In the beginning, I felt guilty
for spending so much time on something not directly related to ministry. I still wrestle with it
from time to time, but it's one place where I don't

have to talk "church" unless I choose to. In the gym I'm just another human being, not a ministry machine/superman. If I want to pray, I can do so even while grunting out that last repetition on the leg press machine.

Furthermore, my time in the gym is the only real contact I have with the world outside of the church that doesn't involve work on behalf of the church. It's both physically satisfying and tangibly rewarding, while most of the rest of my daily routine is mental and emotional and not immediately rewarding. Such contact keeps me out of the "ivory tower" and in touch with real people. And from time to time I do get an opportunity to share the gospel with some curious or hungry soul fascinated by the rare spectacle of a well-muscled and sweaty pastor.

Please understand, I'm not a physician, so accept or reject what I am about to say, depending on whether I make sense to you. My body knows—and my chiropractor confirms—that stress produces toxins which the body has a way of storing in its tissues. Over a period of time these can damage the digestive system, weaken muscles and ligaments and alter body chemistry in ways affecting moods and mental processes, among other things. Stress is particularly hard on the heart and on the adrenal gland. Exercise helps eliminate those stored toxins and aids in restoring healthy body chemistry. It strengthens the heart muscle, helps the adrenal gland begin secreting adrenalin normally again and restores weakened connective tissues, tendons and ligaments. All of this contributes to reduction and elimination of the physical pain and chronic illness so many wounded warriors experience and that their doctors have such a problem diagnosing. it also helps reestablish an overall sense of wellbeing and renews the body's ability to withstand emotional stress and physical diseases.

The procedure I recommend is that you see your personal physician for a complete physical exam in order to determine what kind of exercise you can safely undertake and at what levels of intensity. Since you have depleted your nutritional reserves, ask him to refer you to a qualified nutritionist who can help you rebuild those reserves. I chose to have a hair analysis done through my chiropractor as a means of more accurately pinpointing what nutrients were lacking so that I could eat the proper foods and take the right supplements to gain the speediest recovery possible. It helped tremendously. Others may choose different ways. Find one that works for you.

Then go to an athletic club or gym where good instruction is given. If options are available, shop around and ask questions until you find which club has the best instructors. Tell your instructor about the results of your physical exam, share whatever personal goals you have for exercising and let the professional design an enjoyable program appropriate and effective for you. Understand that, for the first month or more, you may feel ill both during and after your workouts. The exertion may cause headaches. Each of your early workouts will be a burden and you'll want to quit. There will be days when you feel you're just too tired to go. Ignore this. Your body is cleansing itself, and your cells are releasing those stored toxins into the bloodstream where your natural filters can eliminate them. Stick with it faithfully and you'll find yourself a confirmed "sweathog," addicted to the satisfying, full sensation of fatigued muscles. You'll look better and you'll feel better in every way. You'll notice your energy returning in a kind of "body joy" produced by the endorphines secreted by a healthy body when it exercises.

Don't con yourself into thinking you're too far gone or too tired to do this. Exercise is too important to your recovery for you to permit that kind of self-deception. There will be no full and permanent recovery without exercise. It's part of the balance of body and spirit that God intended for us to cultivate.

The Isolation Pattern

What I have to say concerning this pattern may threaten some cherished theologies, but I'm not a bit sorry for it. Most of this section is specifically aimed at pastors, but much of it applies to lay leaders as well.

Most patterns of government extant in the modern church are set up to keep the pastor isolated and to deprive him of power. We don't often realize this and we don't often consciously desire it, but it's true. Most churches today are governed as democracies in which the task of those who occupy offices is to carry out the will of the people as expressed in the vote of the majority. But God's church was never designed to be a democracy carrying out the will of the people. It was intended to be a *theocracy,* ruled by God through His anointed and appointed servants who discern and carry out His will—and who have both freedom and authority to do so.

Because most churches are democracies, rather than theocracies, elders (or their equivalents)—whom God intended to be the pastor's team in ministry—are elected by the people rather than appointed by authority as the Scriptures dictate. In case after case, therefore, they fail to function as the pastor's team in ministry. In fact, they are often elected to their positions by factions opposed to the pastor, in order to place dissenting voices in high places. The results can be devastating as the pastor is effectively crippled in his ability to carry out the vision God has given him for the church.

Further, elders are usually elected for limited terms, after which they are constitutionally required to rotate off the board. Under such circumstances it becomes impossible for the pastor to develop a team of trusted confidants and coshepherds of the flock. Biblically, elders are to be appointed, not elected. Further, in the spirit of Ephesians 4:11, they are born to the task and are themselves gifts to the Church. It takes a lifetime to learn the job! In our modern systems, the moment an elder begins to understand the task, he must step down and allow another "rookie" to take his place.

Please don't confuse this teaching with abuses that have arisen from some quarters of the shepherding and discipleship movement. When domination and control of people arise from a biblical structure, the flaw is in those who hold the positions in the structure, not in the structure. There is a biblically mandated structure for church government, but domination and control is not part of it.

Because we operate our churches on non-biblical bases, we are burning our shepherds out. The pastor today usually stands alone, rather than in the midst of a trusted team with whom the ministry is genuinely shared. Everywhere I go I hear ministers speaking of this isolation, and looking for ways to break out of it. The suggested solution is usually found in fellowship among fellow clergy, but I find this terribly inadequate. There just isn't time enough for the kind of sharing and uplifting needed for this to be effective. I know that for my primary support system to be effective it has to be with me in the daily crush of ministry. I need people who live my own situation with me.

Although I need fellowship with other clergy in order to keep a certain perspective that a layperson can never have, I never feel the isolation any more, as I did in the days when our elders were appointed to limited terms with a compulsory rotation. No matter what crisis we faced, I'd find myself alone. The board seemed paralyzed and unable to learn to minister effectively alongside me with little or no ability to stand firm under fire for the sake of the flock. Everybody suffered for it and the church was weakened.

Finally, after three frustrating, heart-breaking years as a congreation, we changed our form of government to make eldership a lifetime office. We also gave our elders real power to govern, and we tightened the requirements for becoming an elder. We made the office appointive, rather than elective, although we did provide the congregation with a means of nominating candidates and of vetoing any appointees that the other elders and myself might present.

The result was startling. As soon as we were biblically in order, a radical change became evident in the hearts of our elders. Overnight they knew their anointing and were able to walk in it. From that point forth they began to face the crises and to serve the sheep as my partners in ministry. The flock began to look to them as true shepherds. We saw more ministry, more power, more teaching, more stability and more growth as a congregation. They became a group of men with whom I could share my own inner burdens more effectively, and I was never again the victim of professional isolation.

It isn't the purpose of this book to tell you how to change the specific system under which you work, if that system is out of alignment with God's Word. Every situation is unique. I can only say that, under any system, the pastor or anointed lay leader must seek out those called to be close to and safe for him. Gather a team of trustworthy folk and utilize their gifts both in ministry to the flock and for your own support. Ask God to reveal these people to you and then purposefully draw them to yourself. If you're too far gone to do this, then simply ask God himself to sovereignly bring them into your life.

Some of you have been so badly burned and betrayed by trusted confidants and team members that this may seem too difficult—too much of a risk. It seemed this way to me at one time because I, too, had been deeply scarred by people I loved. The truth was that I had chosen the wrong people, and had yet to learn how to identify the faithful and the true. I learned from my failure. I wouldn't want to experience the pain of that failure again, but it was certainly worth it for the fruit it bore in wisdom.

The Self-Abuse Pattern

This pattern is often rooted in a subconscious death wish. Life is a burden and you'd really like to die, so you poison yourself with practices certain to further destroy your already-deteriorating body. The process may be subconscious, or you may have enough awareness to recognize the morbid pleasure you take in it. In either case, it must be stopped.

This pattern is most often manifested in habits of diet and rest. Your eating habits have probably been atrocious. Meal times are irregular. Junk food eaten on the run may be a predominant feature of your luncheon menu. Even good meals are eaten too hurriedly. You overeat. You undereat. Certain food addictions or allergies may appear. As I indicated earlier in this book, you should see a qualified nutititionist and begin to rebuild depleted reserves. Determine to eat regularly. Purposefully eat whole grains and other natural, unprocessed foods. No mystery here. Just good sense. And while you're doing it, remember you're fighting for your life and for God's glory in you.

Rest is really the big issue. Most pastors and lay leaders regularly violate the Sabbath rest. God designed us to function best when we take one day in seven to stop, worship God and do what we ourselves enjoy. That's the law. There is a price to pay for violating that law that's not so much the wrath of God as it is simply the way reality works. If you're a leader, don't expect to accomplish a Sabbath rest on Sunday since that's the biggest workday of the entire week. Choose another day and leave the phone off the hook. Even my elders know not to call me with church business on my day off.

Most of us wounded ones are workaholics

with an average work week running sixty hours at minimum. And we love it so! What noble martyrs we are! For the layperson fully dedicated to ministry, this translates into forty hours at a secular job and twenty or more for the church, all of which takes a toll on the body and the spirit. I frequently find myself running from one set of demands to another at breakneck speed, leaving little or no room for real rest between tasks, much less the kind of meditation in prayer that renews the soul and energizes ministry. Often I'm at my best level of performance when I'm running that way, and I'm loving every minute of it.

The problem is that I'm a lot like the car that rounds a corner at a hundred miles per hour, only to plow into the wall the driver didn't see coming. Suddenly, the resources are gone and I find myself emotionally, intellectually, creatively and physically empty. It's a difficult condition from which to recover. If I can't learn to see the wall coming, then at least I must learn to anticipate where and when it will likely appear and slow down *before* I crash. That means establishing more reasonable patterns of rest and relaxation, even when I don't feel like I'm tired yet. I need to rest *before* I tire, because one inch from the wall often feels no different than ten miles.

By way of breaking the pattern, learn to do simple things like determining not to be the last one to leave the church on Sunday each week. Somehow I must find a way to beat that line of people who feel they absolutely must have five minutes with me on the way out the door in which to pour out the woes of a lifetime—while two-hundred other people clamor for my attention—and get answers worth hours of counseling in the undisturbed privacy of my office. I've begun giving more weight to those little after-church family obligations that arise from time to time, so that I have legitimate excuses to get away by a reasonable hour.

A more effective thing I've done is to give the making of my schedule over to my wife, who is also the church receptionist. She does a better job of telling counselees that I don't have a spot open for three weeks than I do. I feel obligated to them. She doesn't. The whole process creates those little windows of rest in a busy schedule that can make the difference between sanity and insanity.

The Prayer Pattern

Your prayer discipline is probably shot, and if you take a close look you'll probably find that it needed to be. Most of us have been fed a load of legalism about spending an hour a day alone with God. Sometimes it's called "quiet time." Sometimes we call it the "prayer closet." Perhaps you've been taught a certain method for praying. Certain styles of language must be used. You begin with, "Dear God," and end with, "In Jesus' name," religiously. A method I learned in my childhood family was to include "listening" time in my daily devotional. We'd silence ourselves before the Lord and listen for God's voice and/or for

Scripture references to look up. Then we'd record what we heard in a notebook. We called it "guidance," and it was a daily ritual. Maybe you were taught to use a journal. I can remember feeling lost without mine, as if I couldn't really pray without it. Under normal circumstances all that method is good stuff, but in the depth of my wounding it became a lifeless ritual.

At first I felt guilty for spending so little time "on my knees" and I'd strive with all my failing strength to put it back together again. At last the Lord himself told me to stop it. The old pattern, steeped in all those legalisms and methods, just wouldn't work any more. It was no longer adequate for the larger things God wanted to do in and through me.

In the midst of my despair over the absence of refreshment in my quiet time, and for my inability even to maintain the discipline of having one, God said, *"I'll not speak to you as to other men."*

"How then? said I in confusion.

"Trust your instincts," came the reply.

I mulled that over for a while, until I understood that the Lord was trying to rebuild my shattered confidence. But I also realized with a start that nowhere does the eternal Word of God mandate anything concerning daily devotions other than: 1. to "pray without ceasing" (1 Thess. 5:17), and 2. to take in some piece of God's Word daily for the heart to meditate on continually (Ps. 119 and others). Good news! That leaves lots of room for creativity and change.

A long time passed before I again had the energy to block out time for daily devotions. But that was all right, because the Lord began to train into me a new awareness of how to pray without ceasing and to meditate on His Word. Rather than block out time in which to expend energy and force a concentration I no longer could generate, I could simply plant some portion of the Word in my mind and heart and let it resonate there all day long. I found that whatever I put into my heart, I meditated on subconsciously. Insights would float up out of nowhere. My very instincts could be infused with the Word, and I could be more responsive to the need of the moment than I had been previously.

One of my needs, even when I was healthier, had been to steep the entire day more deeply in prayer, rather than relegate it too exclusively to my daily devotional hour. I began to pray more in tongues than in English. The energy expenditure was lower and the return in power was greater. As I made the changes, I found that I became more alive to the prompting of the Spirit in the moment.

Ironically, my traditional daily devotional hour was actually beginning to get in the way of real communication with God. Patterns had taken over where the give and take of real relationships should have been. Since then I've come to know God's presence in a new way. Today I've returned to a disciplined practice of daily meditative prayer, but it has new life and flexibility in it.

So, let God both destroy and rebuild your pattern for prayer and Scripture study, and don't let yourself feel guilty if it seems like you're not praying or studying at all for a time. The feeling will vanish when the newer, more adequate form emerges. Allow for experiment and failure in the meantime.

I realize that much of this chapter sounds like self-help of the sort a deeply Wounded Warrior can no longer initiate. In each case, however, note that what made the difference was an outside intervention, either divine or human or both. Begin breaking patterns by confessing your helplessness, and then call upon the Lord to rescue you. It's a time-honored and proven-to-bear-fruit cry.

If you're ministering to a wounded one, be careful not to ask him for the sort of self-help of which he may no longer be capable. Simply watch for your moment and listen to the Spirit so that you will know when an intervention would be life-saving, and what sort of action would be most effective.

Chapter 7

Living With a
Wounded Warrior

7

Living With a
Wounded Warrior

In my situation my wife escaped most of what I suffered and was able to support me in my recovery. Her invincibly positive nature forms a good counterbalance to my melancholy one and I write this chapter from the wellspring of her wisdom in dealing with me. The basic outline for this chapter is her work. I realize, however, that there are cases in which both husband and wife are suffering third-stage incapacities. For their sakes I've done my best to address their situation as well as my own. Many of the support functions outlined here for a spouse can be effectively shouldered by a close friend, as well.

Let's begin with couples who are wounded together. The most basic temptation you face is to see one another as the enemy. You're no longer able to meet one another's needs. Because normal household pressures aren't adequately dealt with by either of you, they grow from small irritations into large ones very quickly. Chances are you've never been able to be real partners in the sharing of emotions, even in your healthy days. The present situation, therefore, widens a hidden crack into a gaping chasm.

Therefore, no matter how incapacitated you feel, the first mental discipline you must strive to exercise is to identify the real enemy and resolve not to attack your mate. The situation—not your mate—is your enemy. If you can't yet face the situation together and learn to talk out your feelings with one another, then at least learn not to attack one another. I can't give you a multi-step plan for accomplishing this. You wouldn't be able to follow it anyway. I can only say that you must do it by God's grace, directly and simply. Get a trusted third party to help you do it, if necessary, but get it done. I've spent a number of hours interpreting wounded spouses to wounded spouses. It helps.

A Wounded Warrior desperately needs his "space." "Down" time, spent alone, is critical to his recovery, so be prepared to carry more than your share of the weight in the household if he is wounded and you remain functional. He no longer has the capacity to deal effectively or consistently with daily stresses and responsibilities. It may seem to you that he will never rebound from his pain, but he will, unless you compound it with misunderstanding and misplaced pressures.

It will be a lonely time for you while one who may once have been strong limps through a period of weakness. Listen sympathetically to his hurts, fears, depressions and angers, but don't wallow in them with him. At all costs remain positive. He doesn't need the pressure you create by becoming angry with him or by insensitively demanding that he do things to correct his condition or his behavior.

Above all, *believe* in him when he can't believe in himself. Beth used to put herself directly in my face—the only time I could handle the pressure of direct frontal communication—and firmly tell me I was a good pastor, a good father and a good man. I needed to hear it. I knew too well that my performance at home was deteriorating, and I was encouraged as she helped me to hold onto my identity.

Your Wounded Warrior may have lost all faith that God will conquer the situation. If this is the case, your job is to maintain faith on his behalf, no matter how difficult it may seem. The wounded one is hanging on by a decision of his will— "white-knuckling it," if he's hanging on at all—not feeling near to God or even that God is willing to help. If you can believe *for* him, you help rebuild his faith.

If both of you are wounded, then, *as a couple*, find someone outside the marriage to do for you what one of you can no longer do for the other. It may be a time of distance in your relationship and is therefore a vulnerable time. Because of this vulnerability, under no circumstances should you seek help or support individually, outside the marriage, from a member of the opposite sex. I scarcely need to spell out for you the dangers that lie down that path. Find that person or persons together and get help together. Best if you find another couple. Better yet if you have a small group that meets regularly for prayer. "Dump" there together. Let them believe in you and reaffirm your callings as individuals and as a couple.

If you are the whole one and your mate is wounded, do all you can to keep the household running smoothly. Maintain a light atmosphere, happy and orderly. The comfort and the refuge of home are a balm to him. At this point in his life it's too easy for home to become a place of pressure that drives him out of the home in order to find "space." Out of the home, his vulnerability opens him to those who would prey upon his emotional need. Home must be a place where he knows he won't be wounded or pricked. Therefore, if you find your wounded one sitting alone in a stupor, leave him there and deal with the household on your own. He'll be fine and eventually he'll come out of it. You'll only drive him deeper into withdrawal by making demands.

Many times Beth found me sitting at the kitchen table, lost to the world and staring blankly into space. A simple hug around the shoulders with no accompanying demand for response was medicine to my ailing spirit. She would then go about her business praying for me, and I felt it.

If both of you are wounded, you must exercise as much self-control as you are capable of. Again I say that you must strive not to identify one another as the enemy. It may help to learn to recognize when the household pressure is building and resolve to go out together for a while before one or both of you explodes. Get a sitter for the kids and go to a movie or take a walk. Anything to break the pattern and get out of the pressured environment.

In every case in which I have seen two Wounded Warriors attacking one another in a marriage relationship, there were definitely deep-seated problems of another kind at work. Those problems existed long before the wounding from outside the marriage began, and they only surfaced in force when the couple's normal restraining strengths wore thin. By contrast, couples who are whole as individuals seem to survive well even when both are wounded. I believe that when mortal combat in the home accompanies outside wounding, the ultimate source is often a wise and loving God who deliberately aggravates our brokenness so that it can be faced and resolved.

I have seen wounded couples do just this sort of facing of brokenness and survive. In the facing of it, they were healed of old wounds and sins, and then were enabled to recover from their present wounding.

If you are the whole one, cover your Wounded Warrior with a blanket of prayer every waking hour. It will give you a sense that you are helping, rather than standing helplessly by, and real power will be released to mend your warrior's wounds. Don't encourage him in ways that demand performance, and don't tell him what you're praying for. He'll feel obligated to try to make it happen, and that only deepens the wounding.

When both of you are wounded, find someone outside of your marriage to pray this way for you, because you won't be able to do it consistently for one another. Make certain this person understands your condition, and then trust him. As I said before, never seek out that support as an individual alone if you can possibly act jointly. For safety's sake it should be done together. Best if you find a couple. Better yet if you have a small group of trusted friends in Christ with whom you meet regularly. They can share the burden and give much more effective support.

Out in the world, the whole one in the relationship must keep a sharp lookout for what kinds of people are around the wounded one. This is true especially in church where people press in on the leader, demanding ministry with no concept of, or care for, his personal condition. Begin by guarding his heart with prayer. With the help of Father God, be strong in your own spirit and, almost in a mystical way, carry the bleeding heart of your wounded one in your own bosom. Lift his pain to the Father on his behalf. "Bear one another's burdens and so fulfill the law of Christ"

(Gal. 6:2).

For instance, at church one day Beth noticed that a certain person had me cornered and was droning on and on, until I turned sickly gray. She quickly came up beside me and began to listen to what was happening and to feed me in silent prayer. The mere fact of not being alone in the situation was a strength to me.

She also had a sixth sense concerning those who would take advantage of my vulnerability and warned me many times concerning them. I was free to listen or not to listen, and she didn't add to the pressure by demanding that I hear her. She simply stated the facts and then left me alone.

Often she'd head people off by getting to them herself before they could get to me. She'd do it so nicely and subtly that the potential trouble-maker didn't even know what had happened. For all anyone else knew, she was just friendly, happy Beth coming to talk.

Never do this sort of thing in a way that lets the one you're heading off know you're angry or being protective. To do so makes you look bad in their eyes and creates new tensions in the body of Christ that your wounded one will have to deal with later.

When both of you are wounded and in need of protection, I again advise you to alert trusted others to do for you what you may be unable to do for one another. You'll find, however, that even in the depth of wounding, those protective instincts are still active. To a certain degree, you can continue to exercise protective functions for one another, no matter what condition you're in. I think this is so because a threat to your mate is perceived as a threat to yourself. In your wounding, your paranoia keeps alive those protective instincts. Up to a point, those instincts are reliable. The problem for the Wounded Warrior, however, is one of balance and a tendency to carry a sixth sense for trouble beyond the bounds of reality and into delusion. Seek, therefore, to be disciplined enough not to turn the protective words you speak to your mate into demands that must be responded to and use the checks and balances provided by those trusted others I spoke of to control your tendency to lose perspective.

As the functional one in the relationship, be acutely aware at all times that those who wounded your partner were probably trusted friends, people into whom he poured his time, love and energy. He's been stabbed in the back by them, and his heart is cut to ribbons. The problem may not be one of forgiveness. He may already have accomplished that. It's just that emotional woundings are like physical ones. They take time to heal, even after medicine is applied. The process will probably take much longer than you think you can bear, but it does come to an end. Learn patience in the meantime. It is therefore of critical importance that you in no way betray his confidence. Share with no one what he shares with you.

> Let every one be on guard against his neighbor,
> And do not trust any brother; Because every
> brother deals craftily, And every neighbor goes
> about as a slanderer. And everyone deceives his
> neighbor, And does not speak the truth, They
> have taught their tongue to speak lies; They
> weary themselves committing iniquity. Your
> dwelling is in the midst of deceit; Through deceit
> they refuse to know Me, declares the Lord. (Jer.
> 9:4-6)

> Even my close friend, in whom I trusted, Who
> ate my bread, Has lifted up his heel against me.
> (Ps. 41)

Deep wounds from betrayals such as these take years to heal. As you conceal from others what your warrior has shared with you, conceal his general condition as well. In every way help him preserve the image of strong functionality before the world. *No one*, except those the warrior says are all right, need know how he really feels. If asked, say, "All is fine, but you can pray for us; it never hurts." Don't risk giving anyone ammunition that might be used later to add to the wounding. Don't risk damaging your warrior's trust in you. He may have no place else to go, and his trust in you can spell the difference between survival and complete breakdown.

While you are preserving a functional public image, take care not to undermine your partner's self-esteem by taking up too much of the slack he leaves, either at home, at work or in the ministry. Better to lend a little help in the doing of a task than to do it all for him. Better even to let a task go undone than add to his guilt burden by doing jobs that he knows and accepts as his own.

Your own needs will have to be set aside for a while. The warrior in deep wounding isn't capable of meeting them. He'll try, but he really has nothing to work with. Your response to his incapacity can be either healing to him or immeasurably destructive. I know of one wife who— wounded by her husband's incapacity to meet her needs, and not understanding the reason for it— turned to the attack and accused him of hypocrisy in his faith and ministry. She pushed and pushed until he exploded. His raw nerves couldn't take the pressure. To show love, to pay attention to a new dress or to appreciate how well a household task was accomplished, is often beyond his capability. There is simply nothing left to give and no amount of spiritual or emotional grunting on his part will produce it. The Wounded Warrior is fully aware of his failure and the guilt of it is driving him deeper into wounding, but there is almost nothing he can do to change it.

You'll have to learn to draw from the Lord alone what you need to sustain your own emotional health. If you have children in the home, you'll have to find the faith to believe that God knew what shape their wounded parent would be in and that He has already provided for their survival. There were times when I was so "gone" that the very presence of my wonderful children made me want to scream in desperation. Try as I might, I couldn't respond to them as they wanted me to. Their little voices were like daggers cutting my mind in pieces and carving chunks off my already bleeding nerves.

Family members often had to repeat things to me two and three times in order to make their messages understood. I could hear the sounds they made, but my mind couldn't make sense of what was being said. I would ask for things to be repeated again and again until the kids would give up and get Beth to tell me. I can still hear her saying, "Get in his face. Make certain you have eye contact. Ask him if he is listening. Then ask him to repeat what you said. If that doesn't work, come get me."

Beth was wise enough not to criticize me for my inability. She knew what kind of man I am under normal circumstances and was therefore able to give me room to recover. I gave to the children as I could and I knew Beth covered for me when I couldn't. On the whole, however, she tells me I did well with the children. I knew that as children they could never understand what was happening to their father and so I made extra effort.

Through it all Beth learned more deeply than ever how to derive her sense of self-worth and beauty from the Lord. She learned to know when He noticed and when He complimented her at the times when I couldn't. She "embraced her fireball" in the form of her own loneliness—as I embraced mine in my wounding—and let it work purification in her heart. As a result, she outgrew the need for me to supply those things I could no longer supply. Then, when I did begin to recover, and did begin to affirm and to nurture her again, she was delighted, but not dependent.

Most of what I've written here is from the perspective of a man supported by his wife. I need to emphasize that when the wife is wounded and the husband is functional the task is exactly the same. Husband and wife are partners in ministry and the partnership must be defended. It isn't that Beth's and my relationship is more important than our ministry, but rather that our ministry is first to both of us. We minister together in partnership. In fact, our ministry is a big part of why our marriage works so well. We're like warriors who fight back to back, guarding one another from attack even as we advance and take ground from the adversary. When one goes down, the other stands guard so that the partnership is preserved. Neither of us works as well alone as we do together.

For example, in 1984 Beth and I were scheduled to teach and lead worship at a national gathering of the renewal movement in our denomination. Just a few days before our scheduled departure, however, Beth was admitted to the hospital with acute abdominal pain. A day later, surgeons removed a cyst the size of grapefruit from her left fallopian tube. I could have gone on to the meeting and Beth would have been okay in the hospital, but the Holy Spirit wouldn't let me go. I was to stay home and guard my fallen partner for the sake of our ministry together, and so for three days I spent every spare moment sitting in the hospital holding her hand.

I've been amazed to discover how many ministers' wives are suffering at home because of the tongues wagging in the fellowship in relation to the way they believe she carries herself. In many fellowships the minister's spouse does as much work as he does and in nearly every aspect of the ministry. She, too, can burn out in the service of the Lord and needs the same care her husband would need if he were wounded. Unfortunately, too many husband/pastors have no sense of partnership and so neglect the Wounded Warrior on the home front. They often continue to pursue their ministries, all but blind to the plight of their mates.

Finally, in no way take personal responsibility for your Wounded Warrior's recovery. What he is suffering is an issue to be settled between him and his Lord. You can pray, support, love and listen. You can avoid being part of the problem and you can help by creating an environment conducive to healing, but you may not turn out to be a key part of the solution. The solution can only be found between him and his Father God. They're the ones who are arguing. They're the ones who must settle it. Grant him the room to hash it out within himself without joining him in his bitterness, preaching at him or offering unasked-for counsel.

The end result in your recovered Wounded Warrior will be increased wisdom, balance, stability, power and all the fruits of the Spirit. It's worth waiting for.

Chapter 8

Epilogue

8

Epilogue

How long will my recovery take?

Speed of recovery depends on a number of factors. How healthy were you before you sank into wounding? How strong is your general make-up, both physically and emotionally? What kind of support systems are available to you to aid and assist in your healing? What kinds of pressures continue to drain your energies? Is good counsel available? Under any circumstances recovery is a lengthy process. It takes months or even years. So emotionally prepare yourself for a long period of struggle. You've spent resources that are not easily replaced and you must give yourself time to build them up again.

Will I recover completely?

Yes and no. You will probably never fully recover the level of intensity, strength and resiliency you enjoyed before you burned out. Unfortunately, you have squandered an only partially renewable resource and will henceforth and forever be compelled to measure your energies against the tasks that come your way and act accordingly. You will, however, have gained a wisdom more valuable and more life-giving than the resources you lost. You may, therefore, actually become more productive with less expenditure of energy than you thought possible. You will also discover that you are much less easily driven off balance emotionally. Your sense of perspective will have been honed to razor edge.

What about relapses?

You'll have many in the course of your recovery. Even today, if I overextend myself for too long a period of time I may suddenly feel completely undone, as if there had been no recovery at all. I've learned that such episodes mean nothing. Rest and a stronger sense of perspective tend to cure me.

For a time you may feel like a bouncing ball, sometimes in the depths of your former despair, sometimes out. Or you may descend to stage one and then recover quickly, only to plunge to the very bottom a week later. Having done so, you may awaken the next morning wondering what the whole thing was about, after all, because you feel so great again. Remember that recovery takes time and that relapses are part of the process.

What if my mate thinks that all this is just a bunch of nonsense and won't stop putting pressure on me to perform what I can no longer perform?

This is not uncommon among women. Too many husbands don't understand the condition and often don't even wish to understand. Because of this they continue making selfish demands upon the wife's emotional and physical energy, condemning her if she can't produce and ultimately placing her in danger of serious breakdown.

The problem can happen to men, as well, but the victims are most often women. Much of my answer to this one is included in the previous chapter, but I'll add one more dimension here. As a last resort, a temporary separation may be in order until you have had time to regain your strength and balance. The pain of your absence may serve to bring about needed humility and understanding in your mate, and in the process you will find the space you require to begin rebuilding your lost strength.

Put aside any legalisms you may have accumulated concerning God's command that married people should stay together no matter what. You're doing this *in order that* you might be able to remain together. In fact, if you don't get some distance, the alternative may be forced separation in the form of extended hospitalization.

Forget all those misapplied Scriptures about wifely submission. This has little to do with the issue of submission, but rather with recovering enough strength that you are able once again to actively submit, one to another (Eph. 5:21), in effective partnership.

Why did God let this happen to me?

First, I don't know. Second, I'm glad He did. Third, I'd be pleased if He never let it happen again. 'Nuff said.

NOTE: A listing of other books, tapes and records by Loren and Beth Sandford can be obtained by writing to:

Cornerstone Christian Fellowship
3025 E. 16th Avenue
Post Falls, ID 83854

About the Author

Loren Sandford graduated from Fuller Theological Seminary in 1976 and is the founding pastor of Cornerstone Christian Fellowship in Post Falls, Idaho. Prior to opening Cornerstone he served as Director of Elijah House, Inc. in Coeur d'Alene, Idaho where he counseled full-time. While serving the Elijah House he began accepting speaking engagements and he and his wife, Beth, have since traveled throughout the U.S. and Canada speaking for churches and para-church groups.

As the speaking engagements have continued, popular subjects have been: The Transformation of the Inner Man, The Healing of the Family, The Holy Spirit, Strengthening the Body of Christ, and Worship. The enabling of the Body of Christ to minister is a consistent focus.

Loren is the author of *Birthing the Church,* published by Bridge Publishing of South Plainfield, New Jersey. He and Beth have released several cassette tapes and an LP of their music. Beth shares in all the work. They have three children.

OTHER PUBLICATIONS OF INTEREST
FROM VICTORY HOUSE

The Transformation of the Inner Man
by John and Paula Sandford

The most complete text on inner healing—a classic Biblical guide for dealing with inner conflicts.

ISBN 0-932081-13-4 (pa. $7.95)

Healing the Wounded Spirit
by John and Paula Sandford

Going beyond *Transformation...* This book is for all who have been hurt. A searchlight for finding God's healing power.

ISBN 0-932081-14-2 (pa. $8.95)

The Power of Praise and Worship
by Terry Law

Karl Strader says this is the "best teaching available today on experiencing God's power through praise and worship."

ISBN 0-932081-12-6 (pa. $6.95)

Praise Releases Faith
by Terry Law

A book that will unleash God's power in the life of the reader. Provides a foundation for standing against all assaults. A faith builder.

ISBN 0-932081-15-0 (pa. $6.95)

Worship As Jesus Taught It
by Judson Cornwall

Cornwall's newest and best book on worship. Gives new understanding concerning true spiritual worship.

ISBN 0-932081-16-9 (pa. $6.95)

Available at your Christian bookstore or from:

VICTORY HOUSE, INC.
P.O. Box 700238
Tulsa, OK. 74170